10-14-75

HITLER'S IDEOLOGY

A Study in Psychoanalytic Sociology

In this original and important work, Dr. Koenigsberg lays the empirical foundation for the science of psychoanalytic sociology. Beginning with an analysis of Hitler's belief system, his anti-semitism, and his attitudes toward war, Dr. Koenigsberg proceeds to develop a psychoanalytic theory of nationalism, and of the sources of political ideas.

Hitler is studied, in this work, not in terms of the idiosyncracies of his personality, but as an embodiment of certain central trends in our civilization: war; racism; revolution; nationalism. In uncovering the psychological sources of these ideologies for Hitler, therefore, Dr. Koenigsberg sheds light upon the source of their appeal for contemporary men.

Dr. Koenigsberg's analysis is based upon a close reading of Hitler's public statements. He traces the origin and development of Hitler's anti-semitism. He examines Hitler's attitudes toward war, and puts forth a number of hypotheses to explain the motives underlying participation in this activ-

(Continued on back flap)

(Continued from front flap)

ity. Among other topics which are investigated: the role of the death-instinct in Hitler's behavior; the sexual source of Hitler's revolutionary impulse; Hitler's devotion to "the people;" Hitler's violent reaction to the death of his mother, and the importance of this event in the development of his political ideas.

The implications of this work are enormous: Dr. Koenigsberg has provided a method whereby public statements might be used to identify the psychological origin and meaning of political and social events. In so doing, *Hitler's Ideology* defines a path for the development of a psychoanalytic science of culture and history.

HITLER'S IDEOLOGY

A STUDY IN PSYCHOANALYTIC SOCIOLOGY

RICHARD A. KOENIGSBERG

THE LIBRARY OF SOCIAL SCIENCE

New York

Manufactured in the United States of America
Library of Congress Catalog Card Number: 74-84694
ISBN: 0-915042-01-0

Acknowledgments

I wish to thank the following publishers for permission to quote from their works:

Houghton Mifflin Company, Boston, for Hitler's *Mein Kampf*, translated by Ralph Manheim.

Oxford University Press, London, for *The Speeches of Adolf Hitler*, April 1922-August 1939, English translation edited by Norman H. Baynes and published under the auspices of the Royal Institute of International Affairs.

Grove Press, Inc., New York, for *Hitler's Secret Book*.

And to acknowledge the use of material from:

My New Order, edited by Count Raoul de Roussy de Sales, and published by Reynal and Hitchcock, New York.

PREFACE

The present work, it is hoped, constitutes the foundation for a new science: the science of psychoanalytic sociology. The goal of this science is to understand the psychological roots of cultural ideas, beliefs, and values, particularly insofar as these have been embodied in the central ideologies of civilized societies. We hope to achieve this goal through a series of empirical studies, working "from the ground up" in order to establish a base which is solid, and which can be built upon. We may briefly outline, here, some of the central concepts which have emerged thus far.

A *cultural belief* may be defined as a belief which is held in common by large numbers of persons within a given society. We may note two important characteristics of such beliefs. First, they may be viewed as "shared assumptions:" their truth is "taken for granted" by the members of a society; and their espousal is independent of an empirical demonstration of their validity. Secondly, such beliefs constitute powerful forces in a society: they dictate courses of action, both on an individual and a collective level.

Among sociologists, for the most part, cultural beliefs are viewed as "givens," and are used as a means of "explaining" behavior. Thus, according to the concept of *cultural determinism*, the tendency for an idea to be espoused is understood in terms of the fact that it is "symbolically transmitted" from one generation to the next; and the "power" of an idea is understood in terms of the power of group and interpersonal influence. There are a number of fundamental questions, however, which cannot be addressed in terms of this mode of conceptualization. For example: How may we account for the shape and form of specific cultural ideas and ideologies? Why are certain ideas "passed along" and not others? How may we account for the intensity of affect which is attached to certain ideas? Conventional sociological thinking, in short, takes for granted the "content" of culture, and only then can "explain" individual thought and behavior. It is unable, however, to account for the content of culture, that is, to supply an explanation for the nature and shape of culture itself.

It is the goal of psychoanalytic sociology to explore the *determinants of cultural belief systems.* Thus, the psychoanalytic sociologist would ask, not only, "Where did the idea come from?" But also: How may we account for the fact that this idea has been perpetuated? How may we account for the specific form which this idea has assumed? And finally: how may we account for the intensity with which this idea is cathected? It is our view that, in order to answer these questions, one must turn to an exploration of the *psychological roots* of these ideas. We may offer, at the present time, the following theoretical structure in terms of which questions such as these may be conceptualized.

Cultural ideas, beliefs and values may be viewed, we may suggest, as an *institutionalization and social embodiment of primal human phantasies,* phantasies which develop in the context of man's extended period of dependency in the human family, and which reflect certain universal experiences which occur therein. From this point of view: a cultural idea is "passed along" insofar as it has proven to constitute a viable means whereby men may express their phantasies and act them out on the level of social reality; the "form" or "shape" of the ideology reflects the shape of the phantasy which defines it; and the intensity with which a belief or idea-complex is embraced reflects the quantity of affect which is bound up with the underlying phantasy.

The initial goal of psychoanalytic sociology, then, will be to describe the nature of the relationship which exists between cultural beliefs and the phantasies which define and sustain them. We shall attempt to understand the nature of the transformation whereby human phantasies come to be embodied in social forms; and to understand, in turn, the manner in which social forms shape, and provide a definition for, our phantasies.

In the present work we shall examine the relationship between belief and phantasy for a single case: that of Hitler. We shall attempt, essentially, to "account for" Hitler's perception of reality by ascertaining the nature and shape of his phantasies; and by observing the manner in which these phantasies are attached to objects in social reality.

Hitler is appropriate, as a case study, for several reasons. In the first place Hitler possesses a consistent, and highly cathected, belief system. Secondly, Hitler's writings and speeches (which constitute the basis for our analysis) contain an abundance of primary process imagery; this being the case, Hitler's ideas are especially amenable to psychological interpretation. Thirdly, Hitler's belief-system may be considered to be *important* insofar as it was shared by large numbers of persons; and insofar as Hitler's ideas, when acted upon,[1] were to have a profound impact upon world history. We may

---

[1]Hitler's actions, our analysis suggests, *followed as a logical consequence of his perception of reality.* That is to say, once we have reconstructed Hitler's "picture of the world," his behavior, however bizarre, "makes sense" within this framework.

make a further observation with respect to the "importance" of Hitler's ideas.

The central elements of Hitler's ideology--love and devotion to one's country, and a belief that it is important to "defend the honor" of the nation; the identification of a single group within the nation as the embodiment of "evil;" revolution in the name of "resisting oppression;" systematic aggression in the name of "ideals" and in the belief in the "necessity" of such actions--continue to constitute *central parameters defining man's behavior on the stage of world history.* Thus, if we are able to ascertain the psychological roots of Hitler's ideas, we will have shed light upon the dynamics of historical action in the contemporary world.[2]

In the present work, however, development of the implications of our findings has been de-emphasized. I have been concerned, rather, with *establishing psychoanalytic sociology as a science.* To this end I have presented my data and interpretations "quietly," and have avoided speculating beyond the case of Hitler.

I have attempted, further, toward the goal of establishing a *science,* to adhere, in the present study, to the standards of inductive rigor required in the experimental sciences. Thus, I have omitted the inclusion of data, and have avoided making interpretations, which would have been justified had my standard been the "clinical" model in terms of which historical and psychoanalytic studies are usually conducted. This being the case, I would argue that my conclusions, however paradoxical they may appear, however they may contradict conventional modes of understanding, *are essentially conservative.* What is at stake here is a foundation of *definite knowledge,* a base which is solid, and upon which a true science of human ideas, beliefs and values may grow and flourish.

I should like to call attention, finally, to the *tabular form* in terms of which we have organized, analyzed and presented our data. The use of such a form, while uncommon in studies which deal with the kind of material which is dealt with in the present work, may be viewed as serving the purpose which is served by tables in all scientific work: it represents a means of *simplifying* and *clarifying* the data; it emphasizes the *inductive process* whereby conclusions are reached, and permits the reader to identify and to evaluate, in any given case, the evidence which has generated a particular interpretation; it embodies a *quantification* of the data.[3]

---

[2] Psychoanalytic sociology, from this point of view, aspires to serve as a *mode of social enlightenment,* as a means of bringing psychological insight to bear upon contemporary social phenomena, and of introducing the psychoanalytic frame-of-reference into the historical process.

[3] In the present work, the *frequency* with which a given idea or association appears in Hitler's work is viewed as reflecting the *centrality* of such an element within the framework of Hitler's belief-system.

TABLE OF CONTENTS

List of Tables

Abbreviations of Works
Most Frequently Cited

S-I   Baynes, N. H. *The Speeches of Adolf Hitler*, April 1922-August 1939.
           Volume I. New York, Oxford University Press, 1942

S-II   Baynes, N. H. *The Speeches of Adolf Hitler*, April 1922-August 1939.
           Volume II. New York: Oxford University Press, 1942

HSB   Hitler, A. *Hitler's Secret Book*. New York: Grove Press, 1962

MK   Hitler, A. *Mein Kampf.* Boston: Houghton Mifflin Company
           (Sentry Edition), 1962

MNO   Roussy de Sales, R., ed. *My New Order.* New York: Reynal and
           Hitchcock, 1941

RF   Shirer, W. L. *The Rise and Fall of the Third Reich.* New York:
           Simon Schuster, 1959

PART ONE

IDEOLOGY AND PHANTASY

INTRODUCTION

The present work represents an empirical study of the relationship between Hitler's phantasies and his ideology. More precisely: we are interested in examining the manner in which Hitler's phantasies, projected into social reality, shape his beliefs and define the manner in which he perceives the world.

The basic method used in the present study may be outlined as follows:

Statements were extracted from Hitler's writings and speeches [1] insofar as they expressed his *beliefs regarding social reality;* we were especially interested, in the present analysis, in those statements of belief which contained *primary process imagery.*

Each separate *statement* extracted from Hitler's work was classified according to the nature of the belief expressed; or according to the manner in which *primary process imagery* was related to statement of belief.[2]

The final data appears in twenty-one *Tables,* each representing a separate category, each containing a minimum of eight *statements.* The analyses and the interpretations which appear in the text are based upon the data presented in these tables.

We wish to make the following comments on the conceptualization of the present research:

[1] The works used for the study appearing in Chapter I are *Mein Kampf* (1962) and Baynes' two volume collection of Hitler's speeches (1942).

[2] For purposes of simplification, material judged to be not relevant to the category in which a *statement* was presented was eliminated. For example, the sentence, "The purpose of every idea and of every institution within a people can originally and naturally be only to maintain the substance of the people, which God has created, in bodily and mental health, in good order and purity (S-I, p. 441)" reads, as a *statement* (Table 2), "The purpose of every idea and of every institution within a people can . . . be only to maintain the substance of the people . . . in bodily and mental health, in good order and purity."

(1) This study does not represent an analysis of Hitler's character or personality. While it is possible to make inferences in this respect on the basis of knowledge of a man's phantasies, beliefs or perception of reality, we have not been concerned with doing so.

(2) We have not emphasized, in the present study, an examination of Hitler's life. We have, however, focused upon, and have attempted to indicate the significance of, a single occurrence in Hitler's life (the death of his mother by cancer). It is our hypothesis (Chapter II) that this event constituted a major determinant of the nature of the phantasies which Hitler projected into social reality.

(3) Insofar as we have focused upon Hitler's *perception of reality* rather than upon his *behavior*, the present work is not, essentially, an historical study. Since, however, Hitler's behavior follows, in many instances, as a natural consequence of the manner in which he defines and perceives reality, our analysis of Hitler's beliefs constitutes an analysis of the determinants of his behavior.

Chapter I

HITLER'S IDEOLOGY

1. Destructive Forces in the National Body

Table 1 presents statements which indicate that Hitler perceived Germany as a living organism. He views the country as a "national organism (3; also 2, 4, 9)" which constitutes a "substance of flesh and blood (11)" and which consists of the German people (9, 12, 15). He describes the national organism as a "body corporate pulsing with a vital inner life (17; see also 13)."[3]

Table 1. The Country is a Living Organism

Statement Number	Statement	Source Book	Page
1	France was tearing piece after piece out of the flesh of our national body.	MK	133
2	Could anyone believe that Germany alone was not subject to exactly the same laws as all other human organisms?	MK	155
3	Our movement alone was capable of creating . . . a national organism.	MK	329

[3] Insofar as the country is a living organism it follows, for Hitler, that the loss of territory represents the loss of a piece of flesh from the national body (1, 16); that the blood of the national body consists of the blood of the people which constitute it (5, 10); that war causes a "bleeding" of the national body (6, 7); and that economics constitutes "a living process, one of the functions of that body which is the people (15; see also 14)."

4	From a dead mechanism (the state) there must be formed a living organism.	MK	398
5	It will be the task of a folkish state to make certain . . . that . . . an influx of fresh blood . . . takes place.	MK	432
6	An attempt to restore the border of 1914 would lead to a further bleeding of our national body . . . so that there would be no worthwhile blood left.	MK	651
7	In case of a war . . . the German nation (would be) bled white.	MK	659
8	The state . . . is a "volkic" organism.	S-I	85
9	In place of . . . the State--must be set the living organism-- the people.	S-I	188
10	The towns would not exist . . . if the peasant did not fill them with his blood.	S-I	242
11	What remains is the substance, a substance of flesh and blood, our nation.	S-I	433
12	The "living substance," the German people, is a present reality.	S-I	441
13	(The) task . . . was . . . to build up the entire administration (of the state) . . . until it became a close organic whole, pulsing with life.	S-I	486
14	So much blood has been drawn off . . . into German economic life abroad . . . that the circulation has been stopped.	S-I	829
15	Economics . . . is a living process, one of the functions of that body which is the people.	S-I	851
16	The Polish Corridor . . . is like a strip of flesh cut from our body . . ., a national wound that bleeds continuously, and will continue to bleed till the land is returned to us.	S-II	995
17	The German people . . . had become a body corporate pulsing through and through with a vital inner life.	S-II	1253

Table 2 presents statements in which Hitler indicates his view of the purpose of politics. This purpose, very simply, is to "wage a life battle (11)" in order to "maintain the life of the people (7; also 1, 2, 3, 4, 5, 6, 8, 9, 10, 12, 13)."

Table 2. The Purpose of Politics

Statement Number	Statement	Source Book	Page
1	The meaning and the purpose of the state are . . . to assure the life of the people.	S-I	187
2	Above everything stands the purpose to maintain the nation's life.	S-I	188
3	To maintain the people: . . . *that* is the highest purpose in life and the aim of all reasonable thought and action.	S-I	188
4	I would ask you . . . to continue . . . in this mighty task of maintaining the life of Germany.	S-I	286
5	The . . . test of every institution: does it serve to preserve the people or not?	S-I	441
6	The purpose of every idea and of every institution within a people can . . . be only to maintain the substance of the people . . . in bodily and mental health, in good order and in purity.	S-I	441
7	The task which the administration of justice must set before itself is to co-operate in maintaining the life of the people.	S-I	526
8	(The purpose of the National Socialist Movement is) the maintenance of the people's life.	S-I	629
9	To the service of the maintenance of the people's life, (the National Socialist Movement) will devote all its powers of work.	S-I	441
10	National Socialism . . . did not set the State and its organization as the central point in its programme but rather the people and the people's life.	S-I	694
11	Politics is nothing else . . . than the safeguarding of a people's vital interest and the . . . waging of its life-battle.	S-I	780
12	This body formed by the people must . . . secure in the future the maintenance of this body which is the people.	S-I	780
13	Our own task . . . lies in the maintenance, the care, and the betterment of our people.	S-II	1061

The national body, as we have seen, consists of the people (1: 9, 15; 2:

9): they constitute its substance (1:12; 2:11) and its blood (1: 5, 6, 7). The effort to maintain the life of the people, then, may be viewed as an effort to maintain the life of the national body, that is, to preserve the national organism which consists of the German people.

The task of maintaining the life of the people is not, however, an easy one: Hitler perceives the national body to be in the process of being relentlessly attacked by forces which threaten to destroy it (Tables 3, 4, 6, 7). In the course of his writings and speeches Hitler makes a number of statements in which he specifies the nature of the destructive forces which are threatening the life of Germany. These statements have been classified into three categories, as follows: (1) A force of disintegration. (2) A disease. (3) An organism which wishes to consume Germany.

Tables 3 and 4 present statements in which Hitler expresses his belief that the national body is beset by a destructive force which threatens to cause it to disintegrate. He identifies this force as a "ferment (4: 14);" a ferment of decomposition (3: 5, 7, 8, 17; 4: 12); a ferment of disintegration (4: 5); and as a ferment of decay (3: 4); as a "disintegrator of peoples (3: 9, 10, 16);" an element of disintegration (4: 9); and as a "dissolver of human culture (3: 5)." This destructive force is perceived as setting in motion a "process of disintegration (4: 11; see also 3: 3, 11)" which threatens to effect a "disintegration of the body of the people (3: 19; also 3: 6, 22, 25; 4: 2, 4, 7, 8, 13);" a "decomposition" of the nation (3:2; also 4: 3); a splintering of Germany's being (3: 1); a splitting of the body politic (3: 15); disunion (4: 16); chaos (3: 13, 16); and a break up of the established order (3: 16). It threatens to cause the German people to fall to pieces (3: 14, 28); to be torn to pieces (3: 14, 28); to shatter (4: 17); and to be "torn asunder (4: 17; also 3: 21, 26)."[4]

Table 3. The Disintegration of the National Body

Statement Number	Statement	Source Book	Page
1	Our ancestors contributed to (the) catastrophic splintering of our inner being.	MK	89
2	This (is a) period of (the) incipient and slowly spreading decomposition of our nation.	MK	279
3	The Jew has . . . found . . . in our highest state officialdom . . . the most compliant abettor of his work of disintegration.	MK	316

[4] The agency identified as the cause of this process of disintegration (or, perhaps, the force of disintegration itself) is the Jew (3: 3, 5, 7, 8, 9, 10, 17, 24; 4: 1); the communists (3: 15, 16, 20, 21, 13, 25, 29; 4: 4); and democracy (3: 22; 4: 7).

4	The bourgeois parties . . . bore the ferments of decay in their own bodies.	MK	329
5	The Jew becomes a "ferment of decomposition" among people and races, and in the broader sense a dissolver of human culture.	MK	447
6	What had the bourgeoisie done to put a halt to the frightful disintegration (of the people)?	MK	464
7	The Jew is . . . himself no element of organization, but a ferment of decomposition.	MK	655
8	The Jew is a ferment of decomposition in peoples.	S-I	17
9	The Jew is therefore a disintegrator of peoples.	S-I	59
10	The Jew . . . is the demon of the disintegration of peoples, the symbol of the unceasing destruction of their lives.	S-I	68
11	The German people found itself in the midst of a process of dissolution.	S-I	88
12	At . . . the . . . time when the Reich seemed externally to be gaining strength . . . internally the body of the people as such began to dissolve.	S-I	88
13	Germany would dissolve into chaos.	S-I	228
14	If these insignificant critics were to have their way, Germany would fall to pieces.	S-I	232
15	Marxism . . . lead(s) to a weakening of the general body of the people because it builds upon a splitting up of the body politic.	S-I	255
16	There is the small body of . . . international disintegrators of a people who as apostles of . . . Communism . . . break up established order, and endeavor to produce chaos.	S-I	298
17	The Jewish "ferment of decomposition" . . . destroyed . . . the State organization.	S-I	440
18	We live in the midst of a world which is in ferment.	S-I	450
19	This political disintegration of the body of a people must . . . mean the end of every authority.	S-I	453
20	Marxism means the tearing in pieces of the nation, and thus the weakening of the whole people.	S-I	666

21	Bolshevism (intends) to tear the world asunder.	S-I	675
22	Democracy may continuously disintegrate the European states.	S-I	677
23	Weaknesses . . . of the people . . . facilitate the disintegrating attack of the Bolshevist International.	S-I	698
24	The intellectual Jewish class in Germany had everywhere a disintegrating effect.	S-I	773
25	Marxism (is) a conception of the world with disintegration for its aim.	S-I	846
26	A chaos of views and conceptions . . . tore asunder the German people.	S-I	879
27	In the Bismarckian period the entire bourgeois world failed to notice the beginnings of a process which threatened to dissolve the German people once more into its basic elements.	S-II	990
28	The increasingly rapid falling to pieces of the organic structure of the nation . . . destroyed . . . the people's trust in . . . their leaders.	S-II	1154
29	So long as the leaders . . . paid homage to the insane ideas of Marxism, the only result could be the continued disintegration of the national community.	S-II	1154

Table 4. The Prevention of Disintegration

Statement Number	Statement	Source Book	Page
1	No salvation is possible until the bearer of disunion, the Jew, has been rendered powerless to harm.	S-I	42
2	Today the army carries with it the talisman of political immunity against any attempt at disintegration.	S-I	158
3	We want to burn out the symptoms of decomposition.	S-I	240
4	The period of international Marxist disintegration and destruction is past.	S-I	242
5	We will not capitulate before these ferments of disintegration.	S-I	259
6	It appeared . . . important to prevent the threatening dissolution in the political life of the people.	S-I	295

7	The age of parliamentary democratic disintegration is passing.	S-I	502
8	It is . . . necessary . . . to put a stop to that carping criticism which tends only towards disintegration.	S-I	504
9	We must therefore be the enemy of any attempt to introduce into this European family of peoples an element of disintegration and destruction.	S-I	710
10	There has been effected an . . . immunization of the German Reich against all the disintegrating tendencies.	S-I	734
11	In order to bar the spread of this process of disintegration it became essential to . . . establish . . . a separation between the two races.	S-I	773
12	If a new body-politic was not . . . formed . . . which could overcome the existing "ferments of decomposition" . . . then the nation . . . could never rise again.	S-I	821
13	The movement (is) intolerant and pitiless against anyone who shall attempt once more to destroy or disintegrate this body-politic.	S-I	829
14	All the ferments which were destroying the people have been banished.	S-I	846
15	The organisations of disunion and disintegration . . . must . . . be uprooted.	S-II	1134
16	Every attempt to break up, every wish to dissolve, such a community of peoples . . . will suffer shipwreck.	S-II	1364
17	The German Reich as it stands to-day no one will in the future be able to shatter, no one will tear asunder.	S-II	1425

The following passages indicate the immense power which Hitler attributes to this destructive force and his cosmic conception of the threat which it poses.

This attack is levelled against the very substance of peoples as peoples, against their internal organization: it is levelled, too, against the leaders of these peoples, against those who represent each people's own race, against their intellectual life, against their traditions, against their economic life, in a word against all those other institutions which determine the picture of the individuality, the character, and the life of these peoples and States. This attack is so embracing that it draws into the field of its action almost all the functions of life, while no one can tell how long this fight may last.

(S-I, pp. 692-3)

It is only rarely that the life of peoples suffers from such convulsions that the deepest foundations of the edifice of social order are shaken and that this social order itself is threatened or destroyed. But to-day who will refuse to see or even deny that we find ourselves in the midst of a struggle which is not concerned merely with the problems of frontiers between peoples or States but rather with the question of the maintenance or the annihilation of the whole inherited human order of society and its civilizations? The organization of human society is threatened.

(S-I, p. 683)

Not only Germany, but the entire civilized world is perceived to be under attack.

The death instinct has been defined as a force which "tends to separate and disintegrate all objects upon which it operates (Flugel, 1953);" and as a force tending to "dissolve connections (and) to destroy unities (Lampl-de-Groot, 1965)." From this point of view the destructive force which Hitler perceives to be attacking Germany may be viewed as the *death instinct operating upon the national body*. Hitler's effort to prevent Germany from disintegrating, then, may be viewed as an effort to *render inoperative the death instinct*.

How does one oppose the death instinct? In general terms, by encouraging the development of those forces which represent the life instinct. Thus Hitler suggests that if "the negative forces of destruction" are to be overcome the "positive forces of preservation" must be enhanced (S-II, p. 1154). And encourages the "glorification of the national creative will over against the conception of international disintegration (S-I, p. 68)."

How, specifically, does one go about encouraging the development of the life instinct in a national body? Before attempting to answer this question let us briefly examine the concept of the life instinct.

If the death instinct represents a force which tends to dissolve and to disintegrate, to destroy unities in the matter upon which it operates, then the life instinct may be viewed as a force working to bind matter together, to create unity and integration within a living organism (Flugel, 1953; Lampl-de-Groot, 1965).

Freud (1928) has viewed the life instinct as being operative within each organic cell, and has hypothesized that "the life instincts or sexual instincts which are active in each cell take the other cells as their object; . . . they partly neutralize the death instincts (that is, the processes set up by them) in those cells and thus preserve their lives (p. 89)." Thus, we may suggest, the life instinct, by causing cells within the body to be attracted to one another, works to cause the organism to "hold together;" whereas the death instinct, working to decrease the attraction between cells, causes it to "fall apart."

If the country is a living organism, with the people constituting the body of that organism, it would be reasonable to suggest that each individual human being constitutes a "cell" in this organism. From this point of view the enhancement of the life instinct in a national body would consist of a process whereby the "cells" of this body (the German people) were made to be more closely bound to one another, thus increasing the tendency of this body to "hold together." That is, the forces of disintegration (the death instinct) within the national body could be opposed by causing the elements which constitute this body to be so "tightly knit together" that it could not fall apart. Indeed, Hitler's program for the German people embodies this concept precisely.

Table 5 presents statements in which Hitler expresses his belief that it is necessary for the German people to be "bound together" in order to create a national body which is powerful and capable of resisting destruction. Through a process consisting of the "inner welding together of the body of the people (8; also 2, 13, 22, 27)" Hitler hopes to cause the German people to be "fused into a unity (9; also 2, 14)." The goal of this process is to create a "closely knit body (16; also 15, 20, 21, 29);" to "bind into one the strength of the nation (4; also 22);" and to create an "inner unity of will (7; also 12, 18, 16)." If such a process were successful the result would be a "gigantic mighty compressed will (10; see also 17, 30)" and a people which "holds together like a single block of steel (23, 25; see also 1, 6, 24)." Under such circumstances Germany would be invincible (1), and would be incapable of being broken (1, 5, 28) or of being "torn apart (22)."[5]

Table 5. Union as a Defense Against Disintegration

Statement Number	Statement	Source Book	Page
1	A people of citizens will some day arise, bound to one another and forged together . . . , unshakable and invincible forever.	MK	427
2	(We) should weld and fuse together those who have a . . German heart . . . in the fight against the common hereditary foe of all Aryans.	S-I	12
3	The 1st of May can be only a glorification of the national creative will over against the conception of international disintegration.	S-I	68
4	Today we are binding into one the whole strength of a nation.	S-I	150
5	Our people . . . have become one and . . . this unity in Germany will never break in pieces.	S-I	150

[5] The reality correlate, for Hitler, of the wish to see the German people "welded and fused together" involved, apparently, the wish that the German people might "come together," that they might think and act as a single unit. (See Appendix, Table A-1.)

6	If the whole German people now was possessed of the spirit which is in us and in you, then Germany would be indestructible, would represent an unheard of strength through this inner will tempered like steel.	S-I	180
7	The strength of our people . . . lies in our inner unity of will.	S-I	231
8	The end (of party organizations) is the inner welding together of the body of our people.	S-I	232
9	To solve the problems of Germany . . . it was essential . . . to bring the German people into such a form that the millions of individuals could be fused into a unity.	S-I	260
10	Out of the weak will of sixty million individuals there springs a gigantic mighty compressed will of all.	S-I	262
11	As individuals we may perhaps be weak, but taken all together, nothing can break us.	S-I	262
12	To remove our distress, to overcome our weakness, and thus successfully to wage our life-battle in Germany the necessary pre-condition is unity.	S-I	262
13	All classes must be welded together into a single German nation.	S-I	263
14	You must fuse your will with mine.	S-I	265
15	When a nation . . . is composed of elements which which are not . . . homogenous, it is only . . . an iron resolution which can unite it into a single body capable of resistance.	S-I	445
16	When we shall have created for the National Socialist State such a closely knit body . . . this will form an achievement of extraordinary significance for the future of our people.	S-I	487
17	The nation has been united into one outlook, in one idea, and for one common struggle for existence.	S-I	545
18	The Movement . . . has succeeded in bringing the German people out of a condition of extreme internal chaos into . . . unity.	S-I	563
19	The . . . tasks which lie before us can be accomplished only (by a) closely united body.	S-I	623
20	The harder, the more unbreakable this community is, the more easily will it control the great organiza-	S-I	629

tions which are essential for the building up of the
. . . body of our people.

21	Tasks . . . can be solved only by a people closely united into one body.	S-I	635
22	I shall leave to the future leader a people welded fast together, bound up together as with iron bands, a people which can nevermore be sundered and torn apart.	S-I	635
23	The people must hold together as a single block of steel.	S-I	668
24	Either we shall succeed in working out a body-politic hard as iron . . . or else, lacking this internal consolidation, Germany will fall in final ruin.	S-I	825
25	We shall be able to overcome the difficult times ahead of us only if our people holds together like a single block of steel.	S-I	869
26	The whole German nation must once more be brought to a unity of spirit and will.	S-II	1134
27	Men . . . must be thrown into the great melting-pot, the nation, that they may be . . . welded one to another.	S-II	1134
28	We should now attempt to fashion our destiny in a community of the people which nothing shall break.	S-II	1142
29	The people must come together into a single closely united body, for only from such a unity can come the strength to win salvation.	S-II	1158
30	The German people is united in one will.	S-II	1321

One of Hitler's efforts to oppose the forces of disintegration, then, this data suggests, consisted of an effort to cause the national body to be "welded and fused together" in order to create a "tightly knit body."[6] Hitler believed, apparently, that such efforts would decrease the probability that Germany would succumb to the death instinct.

Table 6 presents statements in which Hitler speaks of a "disease" from which Germany is suffering. He identifies this disease as an infection (3, 22, 23, 27, 30, 31, 33, 34); as a plague (10, 12, 19, 28, 32, 43); as a pestilence (23, 28); as a "cancerous ulcer (18, 36);" as a tumor (1, 2); as a canker (3);

[6] One may speculate that the Nuremberg rallies represented an effort, on Hitler's part, to produce a concrete realization of this phantasy. Hitler may have perceived the performers at these rallies, marching en masse and in unison, as constituting a single, unified body. Insofar as this "body of the people" exhibited vigor and strength, Hitler could persuade himself that, indeed, the forces of destruction had been conquered.

and as an ulcer (25); and indicates that, as a result of this disease, Germany is in a process of "decay (7, 11, 14, 16, 20, 21)." He suggests that, if one is to cure this disease, one must disclose its causes (9, 13, 17, 26, 36, 37); and identifies its cause as a bacillus (29, 35, 40, 41), as a virus (4, 8, 13) and as a toxin (6). Finally, he perceives the agents responsible for this disease to be the Jews (12, 19, 23, 34, 35, 43) and the Bolsheviks (32, 33, 41, 43).

Table 6. The National Body is Diseased

Statement Number	Statement	Source Book	Page
1	Brutal determination (is necessary) in breaking down incurable tumors.	MK	29
2	The Austrian state('s) weakness in combating even malignant tumors was glaring.	MK	29
3	The trade union movement . . . wins the highest merit be eliminating social cankers, attacking intellectual as well as physical infections, and thus helping to contribute to the general health of the body politic.	MK	46
4	It is easily possible that after a certain time . . . a search for the alien virus (will be) no longer regarded as necessary.	MK	62
5	It is easier to master a disease (of a national body) which is distinctly recognizable, than one which is chronic, which leads to indifference, e. g., plague versus tuberculosis.	MK	62
6	The longer the toxins remain in the national body (the more likely they will be) tolerated as a necessary evil.	MK	62
7	Here we face . . . forces of decay which in terrifying number soon . . . began brushing up and down the body politic.	MK	154
8	Sometimes (people) tinkered around with the disease, but confused the forms of the phenomenon with the virus that had caused it.	MK	156
9	The cure of a sickness can only be achieved if its cause is known, and the same is true of curing political evils.	MK	226
10	The starting point of this plague in our country lies in large part in the parliamentary institution.	MK	240

11   (Since) the state did not possess the power to master   MK   246
        the disease the menacing decay of the Reich was
        manifest.

12   The masses . . . feel that the mere fact of (the   MK   310
        Jew's) existence is as bad as the plague.

13   (Politicians) tinkering around on the German national   MK   328
        body . . . saw at most the forms of our general
        disease . . . but blindly ignored the virus.

14   At the time of the unification . . . the inner decay   MK   328
        was already in full swing . . . and . . . the general
        situation was deteriorating from year to year.

15   The nation . . . did not grow inwardly healthier, but   MK   328
        obviously languished more and more.

16   The symptoms of decay of the pre-War period can   MK   328
        . . . be reduced to racial causes.

17   Anyone who wants to cure this era, which is inward-   MK   435
        ly sick and rotten, must first of all summon up the
        courage to make clear the causes of this disease.

18   They think that they must demonstrate . . . that   S-I   36
        they are ready for appeasement so as to stay the
        deadly cancerous ulcer through a policy of moderation.

19   The Jew must take care that the plague does not die.   S-I   38

20   If this battle should not come . . . Germany would   S-I   41
        decay and at best would sink to ruin like a rotting
        corpse.

21   You can see in the Reich today . . . an example of   S-I   46
        . . . mortal decay.

22   The 1st of May can be only . . . the liberation of   S-I   68
        the nation's spirit . . . from the infection of inter-
        nationalism, the restoration to health of peoples.

23   Against the infection of materialism, against the Jew-   S-I   108
        ish pestilence we must hold aloft a flaming ideal.

24   The restoration to health of our people must start   S-I   242
        from the restoration to health of the body politic.

25   I gave the order to burn out down to the raw flesh   S-I   321
        the ulcers of this poisoning of the wells.

26   The only way permanently to cure diseased condi-   S-I   463
        tions is to disclose their causes.

27	Infections (in countries) lead to a crippling of intelligence and of the force of resistance.	S-I	677
28	This is the battle against a veritable world sickness which threatens to infect the peoples, a plague which devastates whole peoples . . . , an international pestilence.	S-I	691
29	The international carrier of the bacillus must . . . be fought.	S-I	693
30	If within this community one State is infected . . . that infection . . . is decisive for all alike.	S-I	694
31	In Europe no . . . common life of the nations is possible . . . when amongst their number there are some who are suffering from a poisonous infection and who openly profess their desire to infect others with the same disease.	S-I	694
32	We have a very real interest in seeing to it that this Bolshevist plague shall not spread over Europe.	S-I	707
33	National Socialism has made our people and therefore the Reich immune from a Bolshevik infection.	S-I	710
34	For hundreds of years Germany was good enough to receive these elements (Jews), although they possessed nothing except infectious political and physical diseases.	S-I	738
35	Only when this Jewish bacillus infecting the life of peoples has been removed can one hope to establish a co-operation amongst the nations.	S-I	743
36	It is . . . not enough . . . that I doctor around on the circumference of the distress and try . . . to lance the cancerous ulcer: I must penetrate to the seat of the inflammation--to the cause.	S-I	801
37	Unless . . . this irritating cause . . . is removed no cure is possible.	S-I	801
38	No merely external remedy . . . can remove the malady itself.	S-I	802
39	Time and time again . . . attempt(s are) made to better an impossible situation . . . and . . . every such attempt . . . leads only to an increase in those symptoms which it is sought to remove.	S-I	802
40	Germany (was becoming) a pestiferous bacillus carrier.	S-II	1157

41	We should avoid close contact with the carriers of these poisonous bacilli.	S-II	1339
42	It is a ridiculous undertaking to try to introduce to Germany . . . the disease which we have driven out.	S-II	1358
43	State after state will either fall a victim to the Jewish-Bolshevist plague or must take measures for self-protection.	S-II	1601

Table 7 presents statements which indicate that Hitler believed that the national body was being threatened by an organism which wished to consume it. This organism, always identified with the Jew, is perceived as a "parasite in the body of peoples (4, 7; also 8, 17)" which wishes to "plunder the nation (19);" to cause it to be "sucked dry (18);" and to "break the framework of the people's lives (16)." It is perceived as a "blood sucker" which "attaches himself to the body of peoples (11; also 9, 10, 12);" as a spider (3); as a vampire (13); and as a "will-o'-the wisp" which is "eating like poisonous abscesses into the nation (2)." The Jew is perceived, finally, as wishing to "devour the peoples of the earth (14; also 15)."

Table 7. The National Body is Being Consumed

Statement Number	Statement	Source Book	Page
1	The Jews (are) a people under whose parasitism the whole of honest humanity is suffering, today more than ever.	MK	150
2	Here we face will-o'-the-wisps . . . eating like poisonous abscesses into the nation.	MK	154
3	The spider was slowly beginning to suck the blood out of the people's pores.	MK	193
4	(The Jew) was . . . only and always a parasite in the body of other peoples.	MK	304
5	(The Jew's) spreading is a typical phenomenon for all parasites: he always seeks a new feeding ground for his race.	MK	305
6	(The Jew) is and remains the typical parasite, a sponger who like a noxious bacillus keeps spreading as soon as a favorable medium invites him.	MK	305
7	The Jew (is) a parasite in the body of other nations.	MK	305
8	The best way to know the Jew is to study the road which	MK	308

he has taken within the body of other peoples in the course of centuries.

9	The rage of the people sometimes flares high against the eternal blood sucker.	MK	310
10	(The Jew's) blood-sucking becomes so great that excesses against him occur.	MK	310
11	(The Jew is) a true blood sucker that attaches himself to the body of the unhappy peoples.	MK	312
12	Consider how greatly (the Jew) has squeezed and sucked the blood (of the masses) in the course of the centuries.	MK	313
13	After the death of his victim, the vampire sooner or later dies too.	MK	327
14	(If) the development we are going today . . . continued unobstructed . . . the Jew would really devour the peoples of the earth.	MK	452
15	The . . . heads of Jewry see the approaching fulfillment of their . . . prophecy about the great devouring of nations.	MK	639
16	Men will . . . fall a victim to those who as international parasites and wreckers only lie in wait for the time when they can break up the framework of the people's lives in order to transform the world into universal chaos.	S-I	411
17	(The) international parasite upon the life of peoples has spread itself over the world for centuries.	S-I	691
18	The nation is no longer willing to be sucked dry by these parasites.	S-I	720
19	Jewish parasites . . . plundered the nation without pity.	S-I	743

On the basis of the data presented in Tables 3, 4, 6 and 7, then, it would appear that Hitler identifies three distinct types of forces which threaten to destroy Germany: a force of disintegration; a disease; and an organism which wishes to consume the nation.

Given this conception of Germany's plight, and given Hitler's conception of the purpose of politics (see Table 2), Hitler's goal as a political leader follows logically: to defeat the destructive forces which threaten Germany, and thereby to "save her from death."[7]

[7]This goal is explicitly stated in the following passage: "The German people did not appeal to us in order that through us it might at last be thrust into the arms of Death--it asked of us that we should find a way into a new and better life (S-I, p. 881)."

One may make the following observations with respect to Hitler's wish to "save Germany from death:"

(1) Hitler's capacity to ignore conventional morality may be understood in terms of the importance which he attaches to this wish:

We want to prevent our Germany from suffering, as Another did, the death upon the Cross.

We may be inhumane, but if we rescue Germany we have achieved the greatest deed in the world. We may work injustice, but if we rescue Germany then we have removed the greatest injustice in the world. We may be immoral, but if our people is rescued we have once more opened the way for morality.

(S-I, p. 60)

All the formal fetters which can to-day be imposed on men become immoral directly (as) they fail to maintain the people, because *that* is the highest purpose in life and the aim of all reasonable thought and action.

(S-I, p. 188)

(2) Hitler conceives of the effort to save Germany, it would appear, in terms of a "fight against death:"

Either Germany sinks, and we through our despicable cowardice sink with it, or else we dare to enter on the fight against death and devil and rise up against the fate that has been planned for us.

(S-I, p. 79)

(We are) ready to undertake . . . the fight for the resurrection of Germany and to wage that fight to the end. And that resurrection (can) come only through fighting.

(S-I, p. 882)

(3) And finally, in spite of his pessimistic diagnosis of Germany's condition, Hitler believes, apparently, that his fight to save Germany will be successful:

(I possess) the inner assurance that the fight for this--our people's right to live--will be brought to a successful finish.

(S-I, p. 407)

How does Hitler, looking back upon his political work after several years in power, evaluate his efforts to "save Germany from death?"

Table 8 presents statements which indicate that Hitler believed that, as a result of his efforts, Germany had been "rescued" from death. He speaks of the "resurrection" of the German people (2, 4, 5, 15, 16); of Germany's "revival (9);" and of the "renewal of the body of the people (1; also 12)." He indicates that the nation had "risen again (6, 11; see also 7);" had been "set on its feet once more (13);" had been "restored to health (14);" had been "awakened from her sleep (3; also 2);" and that it now manifested "vigorous life (8)."[8]

Table 8. Germany is Rescued from Death

Statement Number	Statement	Source Book	Page
1	The first of May must symbolize the renewal of the body of a people which had fallen into senility.	S-I	67
2	We had faith in . . . that . . . Germany which then only slept, that lived again, and to-day celebrates its proud resurrection.	S-I	123
3	Many of our number never dreamed of the length of time it would take to awake this Germany from her sleep.	S-I	124
4	I think . . . of . . . those who . . . had to give their lives . . . for the resurrection of the German people.	S-I	159
5	Thus there came the mighty miracle of the German resurrection.	S-I	161
6	Today Germany has in truth risen again.	S-I	186
7	Germany has found herself! Our people is born again.	S-I	208
8	Today we see in Germany vigourous life.	S-I	213
9	Through those who have made their sacrifices . . . we have gained the strength to perform the miracle of the revival of Germany.	S-I	283
10	When we appeal to the nation once more . . . we shall . . . find ourselves faced by a nation that has . . . awakened . . . from its parliamentary trance.	S-I	427
11	Through us and in us the nation has risen again.	S-I	584
12	As you leave this gathering . . . you will take with you the feeling that a people has arisen again: A Reich has been renewed.	S-I	610
13	A nation that was wasting away in dull despair has been set upon its feet once more.	S-I	646

[8] The variability in the manner in which Hitler describes Germany's recovery suggests that he was uncertain as to the precise nature of what had occurred. Had the Reich died, and subsequently been brought back to life (as 8, 9, 10, 17, 21, and 22 would seem to imply)? Had she recovered from an illness or a decline (as 2, 11, 12, 18, 19, and 23 would seem to imply)? Or had she merely awakened from a sleep (as 2 and 3 imply)?

14	We have succeeded not only in arresting the downfall of the Reich . . . but we have restored (the) Reich to vigorous health.	S-I	650
15	Men . . . will say . . . to you in truth we owe the resurrection of the nation.	S-II	1117
16	It is like a miracle that in so few years we should be able to experience a new German resurrection.	S-II	1537

Finally, given the success of his efforts, Hitler expresses a determination to protect his work. In the following passages Hitler would appear to be saying that now that Germany is alive, she shall *stay alive*, and that the National Socialists shall ruthlessly defend her against further destructive efforts:

To-day the Movement has become Germany and Germany will live. He who raises himself against this life of the nation will meet our resolution and on this resolution he will be dashed in pieces whoever he be.

(S-I, p. 233)

It is laughable when such a little pygmy imagines he can stop with a few phrases the gigantic renewal of the peoples' life. If these insignificant carping critics were to have their way, Germany would fall to pieces again, as she fell before. But we can assure them of this: they had not the power formerly to hinder the rise of National Socialism, and now that the people is awake, never again will they plunge it into sleep.

(S-I, p. 232)

(I hope that the Movement) will leave behind it a German body-politic completely renewed internally, intolerant of anyone who sins against the nation and its interests, intolerant and pitiless against anyone who shall attempt once more to destroy or disintegrate this body-politic.

(S-I, p. 829)

2. The Source of Destructive Forces

We may now pose the question: what was Hitler's conception of the *source* of the destructive forces which were threatening the life of Germany. Where did they come from? How, and in what form, did they enter the national body?

Table 9 presents statements which indicate that Hitler believed that destructive forces entered the national body in the form of a "poison (1-23)." This poison had been "injected into the heart of the people (15; also 3, 4, 14)" and was able to "penetrate the bloodstream . . . unhindered and do its work (18)."[9]

[9] The agency identified as the source of this poison is the Jew (5, 8, 10); Bolshevism (19, 21, 22); the press (14, 15, 18); Marxism (9, 13); enemy propaganda (12); and foreign nations (1).

Table 9. The National Body is Being Poisoned

Statement Number	Statement	Source Book	Page
1	The poison of foreign nations gnawed at the body of our nationality.	MK	15
2	The rats that politically poison our nation gnaw . . . from the heart and memory of the broad masses.	MK	31
3	Day by day . . . the poison (is) poured into the people by bucketfulls.	MK	33
4	It seemed as though a continuous stream of poison was being driven into the outermost blood vessels of this once heroic body by a mysterious power.	MK	154
5	The time had come to take steps against the . . . Jewish poisoners of the people.	MK	169
6	Running parallel to the . . . contamination of the people there had been . . . a no less terrible poisoning of the health of the national body.	MK	259
7	All great cultures of the past perished . . . from blood poisoning.	MK	289
8	(The Jew) poisons the blood of others.	MK	316
9	The bourgeois world itself was inwardly infected with the deadly poison of Marxist ideas.	MK	329
10	The racial poisoning of our national body creates a cultural decline.	MK	392
11	Every year these formations, called states, take into themselves poison elements which they can scarcely ever overcome.	MK	439
12	The poison of enemy propaganda had deprived the people of any sense.	MK	464
13	The first requirement was always the elimination of the Marxist poison from our national body.	MK	680
14	The organized Press . . . ceaselessly pours new poison into the hearts of these peoples.	S-I	32
15	The German press . . . dish(ed) out to the people . . . the worst poison that can . . . be imagined, the worst	S-I	64

kind of pacifism injected into the heart of our people.

16	We will not pause . . . until the last trace of this poison is removed from the body of our people.	S-I	117
17	We want to burn out this whole poison which . . . has flowed into our life.	S-I	240
18	The poison (of the Jewish newspapers) was able to penetrate the bloodstream of our people unhindered and do its work.	S-I	246
19	If a single people in Western or Central Europe were to succumb to Bolshevism, this poison would spread.	S-I	667
20	Democracy is the canal through which Bolshevism lets its poisons flow into the . . . countries.	S-I	677
21	There must be an immunization of the peoples against this poison.	S-I	693
22	National Socialism has sought to remove from the organism of our people those weaknesses which might have favoured the inflow of Bolshevist poisons.	S-I	694
23	I consider Bolshevism the most malignant poison that can be given to a people.	S-II	1339

Table 10 presents statements in which Hitler expresses his belief that the German people are *threatened by sexual contamination.* He attempts to alert the German people to the danger of sexual temptations and impurities in public life (6, 8, 11, 12, 14, 15); to the necessity of combating prostitution (3, 5) and syphilis (3, 4, 7, 9, 10, 15);[10] and to the negative consequences of the seduction of German girls by Jews (1, 15, 16, 17, 18, 19).

[10]Hitler's thoughts regarding syphilis are expressed in the following passage: "There must be no half-measures (in the medical struggle against the plague); the gravest and most ruthless decisions will have to be made. It is a half-measure to let incurably sick people steadily contaminate the remaining healthy ones. This is in keeping with the humanitarianism which, to avoid hurting one individual, lets a hundred others perish. The demand that defective people be prevented from propagating equally defective offspring is a demand of the clearest reason and if systematically executed represents the most humane act of mankind. It will spare millions of unfortunates undeserved sufferings, and consequently will lead to a rising improvement of health as a whole. The determination to proceed in this direction will oppose a dam to the further spread of venereal disease. For, if necessary, the incurably sick will be pitilessly segregated--a barbaric measure for the unfortunate who is struck by it, but a blessing for his fellow man and posterity (MK, p. 155)." One may speculate that the concentration camps had their origin in thoughts such as these. Thus, in the preceding passage, Hitler states that, in order to conquer syphilis, the "incurably sick" will be "pitilessly segregated." While acknowledging that such an action is a "barbaric measure for the unfortunate who is struck by it," Hitler views it to be a "blessing for his fellow man and posterity."

Table 10. Sexual Threats

Statement Number	Statement	Source Book	Page
1	Bear in mind the devastations which Jewish bastardization visits on our nation each day, and consider that this blood poisoning can be removed from our national body only after centuries.	MK	126
2	A disregard of the natural requirements for marriage in our nobility has led to a poisoning of the blood.	MK	247
3	The cause (of) . . . this plague (syphilis) lies . . . in our prostitution of love.	MK	247
4	The moral devastations which accompany this degeneracy (syphilis) suffice to destroy a people slowly but surely.	MK	247
5	Our big city population is growing more and more prostituted in its love life.	MK	248
6	Our children . . . in particular are the sad product of the irresistably spreading contamination of our sexual life.	MK	249
7	Which people will be the first and only one to master this plague (syphilis) by its own strength, and which nations will perish from it.	MK	249
8	What was done to check the contamination of our youth . . . , to attack the infection of our love life . . . (and) to combat the resulting syphilization of our people.	MK	249
9	The question of combating syphilis should have been made to appear as *the* task of the nation.	MK	250
10	(Since) our whole public life today is like a hothouse for sexual ideas and stimulations . . . a struggle against the poisoning of the soul must begin.	MK	254
11	Anyone who wants to attack prostitution must . . . clear away the filth of the moral plague of big-city civilization.	MK	255
12	Theater, art, literature, cinema, press, posters and window displays must be cleansed of all manifestations of our rotting world.	MK	255
13	Public life must be freed from the stifling perfume of our modern eroticism.	MK	255
14	With satanic joy in his face, the black-haired Jewish	MK	325

youth lurks in wait for the unsuspecting girl whom he
defiles with his blood, thus stealing her from her people.

15	(The Jew) systematically ruins women and girls.	MK	325
16	If physical beauty were today not forced entirely into the background by our foppish fashions, the seduction of hundreds of thousands of girls by bow-legged, repulsive Jewish bastards would not be possible.	MK	412
17	Systematically these black parasites of the nation defile our inexperienced young blond girls.	MK	562
18	The ice-cold calculation of the Jew is to begin bastardizing the European continent . . . and to deprive the white race of the foundations for a sovereign existence through infection with lower humanity.	MK	624

We may hypothesize that the fear of sexual contamination is linked to the fear of poisoning. That is to say, we may suggest that "poison," for Hitler, symbolizes the sexual substance, sperm, and that, therefore, the introduction of this substance into the national body is viewed as representing a form of sexual contamination.

Table 11 presents statements in which Hitler expresses his belief in the importance of maintaining the purity of the "blood" and of the race. He speaks of the necessity of taking care of the blood (14); of being "conscious" of the blood (7); and of maintaining the purity of the blood (2, 4, 8, 10, 16); and describes the negative consequences of changes in the blood (18); blood mixture (2, 3); contamination of the blood (12, 14); and defilement of the blood (2). He speaks of the necessity of maintaining the purity of the race (7, 9, 11); and describes the negative consequences of racial pollution (15); the lowering of the racial level (3, 6); the "desecration of the race (1);" and the "destruction of racial foundations (5, 13)." He perceives the lost purity of the blood to be the cause of the destruction of men, nations and culture (1, 3, 4, 13, 16); and suggests that the loss of purity of the blood "destroys inner happiness forever (and) plunges man into the abyss for all time (8)."[11]

Table 11. Purity

Statement Number	Statement	Source Book	Page
1	Blood sin and the desecration of the race are the original sin in this world and the end of a humanity which surrenders to it.	MK	249

[11] This data suggests that Hitler equated "race" with the blood of the national body. In this context Hitler states: "The state (is) a vessel and the race its content (MK, p. 93)."

2	The Germanic inhabitant of the American continent, who has remained racially pure and unmixed, rose to be master of the continent (and) . . . will remain master as long as he does not fall victim to defilement of the blood.	MK	286
3	Blood mixture and the resultant drop in the racial level is the whole cause of the dying out of old cultures.	MK	296
4	Men do not perish as a result of lost wars, but by the loss of that force of resistance which is contained only in pure blood.	MK	296
5	With every means (the Jew) tries to destroy the racial foundations of the people.	MK	325
6	(The Jew) tries systematically to lower the racial level by a continuous poisoning of individuals.	MK	325
7	A racially pure people which is conscious of its blood can never be enslaved by the Jew.	MK	325
8	The lost purity of the blood alone destroys inner happiness forever, plunges man into the abyss for all time, and the consequences can never more be eliminated from body and spirit.	MK	327
9	Peoples which renounce the preservation of their racial purity renounce with it the unity of their soul.	MK	338
10	There is only one holiest human right, and this right is at the same time the holiest obligation: to see to it that the blood is preserved pure.	MK	402
11	The folkish state must take care to keep (the race) pure.	MK	403
12	This contamination of our blood, blindly ignored by hundreds of thousands of our people, is carried on systematically by the Jew today.	MK	562
13	The Jew destroys the racial foundations of our existence and thus destroys our people for all time.	MK	565
14	It requires all the force of a young missionary idea . . . to free (the people) from the snares of this international serpent (Bolshevism), and to stop the inner contamination of our blood.	MK	622
15	Racial pollution (is) the original sin of humanity.	MK	624
16	The impotence of nations, their own death from old age, arises from the abandonment of their blood purity.	MK	662
17	In so far then as we devote ourselves to the care of our own blood . . . we are at the same time doing our best	S-I	481

> to help to safeguard other peoples from diseases which
> spring from race to race.

18   (The) inner value which determines the life of a people   S-I   782
can be destroyed by nothing save only through a change
in the blood.

This data permit one to suggest a further hypothesis: Hitler's fear that the German people will lose the purity of their blood is equivalent to his fear that "poison" will enter the national body, and contaminate it thereby. It follows that, insofar as contamination is viewed in sexual terms, the wish to maintain the purity of German blood is equivalent to the wish to preserve the *sexual purity* of the German people.

Evidence explicitly indicating the *sexual nature* of blood poisoning--and explicitly linking poisoning, sexual contamination, and the loss of the purity of the blood--appears in the following passages:

> With satanic joy in his face, the black-haired Jewish youth lurks in wait for the unsuspecting girl whom he defiles with his blood, thus stealing her from her people. With every means he tries to destroy the racial foundations of the people he has set out to subjugate. Just as he himself systematically ruins women and girls, he does not shrink back from pulling down the blood barriers for others, even on a large scale. It was and it is Jews who bring Negroes into the Rhineland, always with the same secret thought and clear aim of ruining the hated white race by the necessarily resulting bastardization, throwing it down from its cultural and political height, and himself rising to be its master.
>
> For a racially pure people which is conscious of its blood can never be enslaved by the Jew. In this world he will forever be master over bastards and bastards alone.
>
> And so he tries systematically to lower the racial level by a continuous poisoning of individuals.
>
> (MK, p. 325)

> Bear in mind the devastations which Jewish bastardization visits on our nation each day, and consider that this blood poisoning can be removed from our national body only after centuries, if at all; consider further how racial disintegration drags down and often destroys the last Aryan values of our German people, so that our strength as a culture-bearing nation is visibly more and more involved in a regression and we run the risk, in our big cities at least, of reaching the point where southern Italy is today. Systematically these black parasites of the nation defile our inexperienced young blond girls and thereby destroy something which can no longer be replaced in this world. Both, yes, both Christian denominations look on indifferently at this desecration and destruction of a noble and unique living creature, given to the earth by God's grace.
>
> (MK, p. 652)

The data appearing in the present section suggest, then, that Hitler perceived the destructive forces as having, ultimately, a *sexual source.*[12]

---

[12] Hitler's preoccupation with syphilis, within the framework of this interpretation, may be viewed as symbolizing his belief that the disease from which Germany is suffering (see Table 6) is sexual in origin.

Thus, according to this view, Hitler's efforts to maintain German purity may be viewed as representing an effort to *prevent destructive forces from entering the national body.*

3. The Struggle Against Submission

Table 12 presents statements indicating Hitler's perception of weakness in the German people. He identifies weaknesses in the German character and will (3, 4, 9, 11, 13, 20, 21); tendencies toward obsequiousness and servility (5, 6, 7); tendencies toward pacifism (2, 10, 17, 19); a tendency toward the adoption of a self-debasing posture in relations with enemies (1, 2, 8, 10, 12, 14, 15, 16, 18, 10); and inferiority complexes (22, 23).

Table 12. German Weakness

Statement Number	Statement	Source Book	Page
1	A man couldn't help feeling ashamed to be a German when he saw . . . this wretched licking of France's boots.	MK	54
2	Our German pacifist will accept in silence the bloodiest rape of our nation.	MK	112
3	(The) results (of German education) were not strong men, but compliant "walking encyclopedias," as we German were generally looked upon . . . before the War.	MK	237
4	People liked the German because he was easy to make use of, but respected him little, precisely because of his weakness of will.	MK	237
5	Compliance became really disastrous . . . when it determined the sole form in which the monarch could be approached; that is, never to contradict him, but to agree to anything and everything that his Majesty condescends to do.	MK	237
6	The monarchic institution was one day bound to perish from all (the) crawling.	MK	237
7	This servility . . . was a flaw in our whole education, for which we suffered most terribly.	MK	239
8	With a single frightful blow this class (the national intelligentsia), which only a short time before was still governing, is stretched on the ground and with trembling cowardice suffers every humiliation at the hands of the ruthless victor.	MK	331

9	Germany became defenseless, not because arms were lacking, but because the will was lacking to guard the weapon for national survival.	MK	332
10	Blinded pacifists today hope to gain by begging, whining, and whimpering . . . a peace supported . . . by the palm branches of tearful, pacifist female mourners.	MK	396
11	This Republic is liked by the rest of the world . . . just as every weakling is considered more agreeable by those who need him than a rough man.	MK	425
12	Our German people . . . today lies broken and defenseless, exposed to the kicks of all the world.	MK	411
13	We German have been . . . lacking in any will power and determination.	MK	431
14	The state . . . on November 9, 1918, unconditionally crawled on its belly before Marxism.	MK	535
15	Who, then, will be surprised that . . . the rest of the world sees in . . . our people . . . only a stooge, an obsequious dog, who gratefully licks the hands that have just beaten him.	MK	633
16	We humiliated ourselves morally . . . , destroyed our own honour and helped to befoul, besmirch, and to deny everything which we previously held as sacred.	S-I	5
17	To be a Pacifist argues a lack of conviction, a lack of character . . . ; for the Pacifist is indeed ready enough to claim the help of others, but himself declines to defend himself.	S-I	66
18	The character of the November-Republic (consists of) subserviency towards the enemy . . . , surrender of . . . human dignity, pacifist tolerance of every indignity, readiness to agree to everything until nothing more remains.	S-I	81
19	Pacifism as the idea of the State . . . (is) good enough to unman the people.	S-I	82
20	From the internal weakness of the Reich sprang its undignified attitude towards the world without.	S-I	294
21	One half of our political figures consist of extremely sly, but equally spineless elements which are hostile to our nation to begin with, while the other is composed of good natured, harmless, and easy going soft-heads.	S-I	651
22	(People of an earlier time) intentionally inoculated our people that it was inferior throughout, incapable of great	S-II	1095

deeds and not worthy of the rights which belong to all others.

| 23 | Inferiority complexes were artificially cultivated, because they corresponded to the inferiority of those parties who led the nation astray during so many years. | S-II | 1095 |

Table 13 presents statements in which Hitler advocates methods of dealing with weakness. He recommends the espousal of a cause (1, 10), the hardening of body and character (2, 5, 7, 8, 11) and the discouragement of dependency (3, 6, 8) as a means of enabling Germany to overcome her inferiority complex (9) and to gain self-confidence (4, 12).

Table 13. Responses to Weakness

Statement Number	Statement	Source Book	Page
1	A man who is prepared to stand up for a cause will never and can never be a sneak and a spineless lickspittle.	MK	238
2	The state--must organize its educational work that young bodies are treated expediently in their earliest childhood and obtain the necessary steeling for later life.	MK	409
3	The state . . . must above all prevent the rearing of a generation of hothouse plants.	MK	409
4	The German people . . . need that suggestive force that lies in self-confidence.	MK	411
5	Through his physical strength and dexterity . . . the young national comrade . . . must recover his faith in the invincibility of his whole people.	MK	411
6	School (must devote itself to) the discouragement of whining complaints, of bawling, etc.	MK	416
7	Our conviction is that . . . it is only from the fighting spirit that there can come the force which shall master those weaknesses which . . . cripple our people.	S-I	189
8	We ask of you to be hard, German youth, and to make yourselves hard! We cannot use a generation of "mother's boys," of spoiled children.	S-I	547
9	In order to become a great world power (our) inferiority complex must be overcome.	S-I	603
10	Those who . . . are called upon to care for the Party . . . must give to (these) organizations a backbone of National Socialist doctrine.	S-I	629

| 11 | This people . . . (needs) the spirit of proud self-reliance, manly defiance, and wrathful hatred. | S-I | 632 |
| 12 | We wish to reawake in our nation both self-consciousness and self-confidence. | S-II | 1095 |

Table 14 present statements in which Hitler expresses his belief that the Jews wish to attack and to dominate Germany.

Table 14. Jewish Domination

Statement Number	Statement	Source Book	Page
1	The Jew robbed the whole nation and pressed it beneath his domination.	MK	193
2	The Jew is not the attacked but the attacker.	MK	323
3	The press . . . hammers away at the characters of all those who will not bow down to the Jewish presumption to dominate.	MK	323
4	Our internationally minded comrades . . . , in their natural primitiveness . . . , are more inclined to the idea of violence, and . . . their Jewish leadership is . . . brutal and ruthless. They will crush any German resurrection just as they once broke the backbone of the German army.	MK	334
5	Wherever in the world we read of attacks against Germany, Jews are the fabricators.	MK	623
6	Once (the Jews) have achieved . . . economic and political influence . . . they begin to destroy with ever-greater rapidity, until they have turned one state after another into a heap of rubble on which they can then establish the sovereignty of the eternal Jewish Empire.	MK	624
7	It is the inexorable Jew who struggles for his domination over the nations.	MK	651
8	Our Jewish foe . . . (is) a foe to whom we had done no harm, but who none the less sought to subjugate our German people and make of it its slave.	S-II	1264

Table 15 presents statements in which Hitler expresses his determination to prevent the German people from being dominated, exploited or oppressed. He advocates a struggle against oppression (1, 2, 3, 4, 5, 6, 7, 9, 11, 14); affirms an unwillingness to permit Germany to be dominated, exploited or humiliated (12, 18, 19, 20, 21, 23, 24, 25, 27, 28, 31); and expresses a wish to defend Germany's honour (20, 22, 26, 29, 33) and to win freedom for her (1, 8, 10, 11, 13, 15, 16, 17, 26, 27, 30).[13]

Table 15. Resisting Oppression

Statement Number	Statement	Source Book	Page
1	When in . . . 1919 the German people was burdened with the peace treaty, we should have been justified in hoping that precisely through this instrument of boundless repression the cry for German freedom would have been immensely promoted.	MK	632
2	In the boundlessness of (the Treaty of Versaille's) oppression, the shamelessness of its demands, lies the greatest propaganda weapon for the reawakening of a nation's dormant spirits of life.	MK	632
3	With . . . propagandist exploitation of (the) sadistic cruelties (of the treat of Versailles) the indifference of a people might have been raised to indignation, and indignation to blazing fury.	MK	632
4	No nation can remove (the) hand (of the Jew) from its throat except by the sword.	MK	651
5	Only the assembled and concentrated might of a national passion rearing up in its strength can defy the international enslavement of peoples.	MK	651
6	There are but two alternatives: either "Remain quiet and become slaves," or Resistance.	S-I	9
7	If a people is to become free it needs pride and will-power, defiance, hate, hate, and once again hate.	S-I	44
8	The (Nazi) banner . . . will be hoisted over the whole of Germany on the day which shall mark the liberation of our whole people.	S-I	44
9	He who will not be a hammer must be an anvil. An anvil are we today, and that anvil will be beaten until out of the anvil we fashion once more a hammer, a German sword.	S-I	57
10	We . . . make the highest demands upon everyone . . . in order that we may give back to him . . . freedom and the respect of the rest of the world.	S-I	62

[13] It may be observed that the language used by Hitler, here, is entirely in the tradition of revolutionary liberation movements.

| 11 | We wanted to create in Germany the conditions which alone make it possible that we should be freed from the iron fist of our enemies. | S-I | 109 |

1881269

12	We wanted our people to be incited to revolt against the threat of enslavement, we wished that at last the time should come when we should cease to endure like patient sheep one slap in the face after another.	S-I	109
13	We shall know freedom once more in Germany only when we have destroyed the foes of freedom.	S-I	248
14	In the education to resistance we see the condition for the assertion of our life.	S-I	259
15	From the National Socialist . . . struggles alone real freedom gradually came.	S-I	595
16	For the present we have a splendid goal: the freedom of our people.	S-I	618
17	Our task (is to) liberate Germany.	S-I	618
18	The word "capitulation" must never find a place in our dictionary. It is always better to be destroyed in honour than voluntarily to submit to the foe.	S-I	639
19	If anyone should think that he can treat us as slaves he will find that we are the most stubborn people in the world.	S-I	649
20	We are . . . now in a position to ensure that Germany shall no longer suffer robbery and violence.	S-I	720
21	We must . . . firmly proclaim: you can do what you like but you will never compel us to recognize a yoke.	S-II	1021
22	Never will I do anything to violate my own honour and the honour of the nation.	S-II	1121
23	We wish to champion our home-land which we refuse to see dishonoured and insulted.	S-II	1121
24	We can never permit our people to be humiliated and treated as a slave.	S-II	1137
25	The world must learn that the time is past when the German people could be oppressed, subjugated, and dishonoured, and, further, that that time will never return.	S-II	1150
26	However unqualified our love of peace . . . we will with	S-II	1179

the utmost fanaticism defend the freedom of Germany
and the honour of our people.

27	We are resolved to stand without a moment's hesitation upon our feet if the world demands from us anything unworthy.	S-II	1205
28	To everyone we say that he who wishes to rob the German people of its freedom can do that only by violence and . . . against that violence we shall defend ourselves.	S-II	1206
29	Never will I . . . set the nation's signature to a document which means the voluntary surrender of Germany's honour.	S-I	1206
30	It is the fairest fight, the most glorious task that could be set before a mortal man--to champion the cause of a people which lies in humiliation, which men insult, whose honour they think they can trample underfoot.	S-II	1315
31	One people are we and no one can break us: one people we remain and no world can ever subjugate us.	S-II	1331
32	Come what may, Germany will stand firm, she will not bow, she will never again submit.	S-II	1331
33	You have returned into a mighty new Germany, that once again knows conceptions of honour, whom nothing can overthrow.	S-II	1588

The data presented in these four Tables may be summarized, simply, as
follows: Hitler perceives the German people to be weak; and advocates a
struggle to overcome weakness. Hitler perceives the German people to be
threatened by the wish of her enemies to dominate, exploit and to humiliate
her; and advocates a struggle to prevent the actualization of this wish.

One may suggest that the struggle against weakness and the struggle
against oppression may be viewed, within a psychological frame-of-reference,
as possessing a common denominator. That is to say, one may view each of
these struggles as being motivated by the wish to enable the German people
to *avoid falling into a posture of passive submission.* In the first instance the
struggle consists of a struggle against *tendencies within the German people
predisposing them toward the adoption of such a posture* (i. e., their
tendencies toward weakness, servility, pacifism, self-debasement, etc.). In the
second instance the struggle consists of a struggle against those *agencies
which wish to force the German people to adopt such a posture* (i. e., by
attempting to attack her, dominate her, humiliate her, etc.).

We may suggest a further interpretation: Hitler's fear that the German
people will fall, or be pushed into a "posture of passive submission" is
equivalent to his fear that the German people will succumb to sexual
seduction, and suffer contamination thereby (see previous section). Thus,

according to this view, Hitler's perception of the German people is that of a woman who is in danger of permitting sexual seduction to occur: [14] he believes that others wish to dominate her, to exploit her, and to destroy her honor (Table 15); he fears for her because of her "weakness of will (Table 12);" and, finally, he fears that she will permit the sexual substance to enter her body (Table 9), thereby causing her to suffer sexual contamination (Table 10) and to lose her purity (Table 11).

This interpretation is supported by the passages which appear below, in which Hitler equates a posture of passive submission with the introduction of a "drop of poison" into the bloodstream.

> A shrewd victor will, if possible always present his demands to the vanquished in installments. And then, with a nation that has lost its character--and this is the case of every one which voluntarily submits--he can be sure that it will not regard one more of these individual oppressions as an adequate reason for taking up arms again. Clausewitz . . . singles out this idea and nails it fast . . . , when he says: "That the stain of a cowardly submission can never be effaced; that this drop of poison in the blood of a people is passed on to posterity and will paralyze and undermine the strength of later generations."
>
> (MK, p. 668)

> Only cowards give themselves up, and that cowardice works on and spreads like a drop of poison stealing through the body. And thus one comes to recognize that it is always better if necessary to accept an end with dread than to suffer a dread which has no end.
>
> (S-I, p. 151)

> Once the disgraceful armistice had been signed, neither the energy nor the courage could be summoned suddenly to oppose resistance to our foes' repressive measures, which subsequently were repeated over and over. But the more of these individual dictates had been signed, the less justified it seemed, because of a *single* additional extortion or exacted humiliation, to do the thing that had not been done because of so many others: to offer resistance. For this is the "drop of poison" of which Clausewitz speaks: the spinelessness which once begun must increase more and more and which gradually becomes the foulest heritage, burdening every future decision. It can become a terrible lead weight, a weight which a nation is not likely to shake off, but which finally drags it down into the existence of a slave race.
>
> (MK, p. 670)

Hitler's belief that "cowardly submission" is equivalent to the acceptance of a "drop of poison" into the bloodstream is based, we may suggest, upon the sexual meaning which Hitler assigns to the act of submission. [15] That is to

[14] One may note, in this context, the following statements: "The people in their overwhelming majority . . . are feminine by nature and attitude (MK, p. 183)." "(The masses are) like the woman (who) would rather bow to a strong man than dominate a weakling (MK, p. 42)."

[15] See also Table 13. The manner in which Hitler describes German "weakness" suggests that he viewed it in terms of the adoption of a masochistic sexual posture (1, 2, 6, 8, 12, 14, 18); and in terms of an unwillingness to resist the adoption of such a posture (1, 2, 4, 9, 13, 15, 16, 18, 20).

say, to "submit," for Hitler, is to adopt a passive sexual posture, and, consequently, is to permit the introduction of the sexual substance into one's body.[16]

4. The Union of Austria and Germany

Table 16 presents statement in which Hitler expresses his attitude toward the alliance between Germany and the Habsburg rulers of Austria. He states that this "unholy alliance (7)" had been the "ruin" of Germany (37) and that it would lead to her "fatal collapse (33)." He indicates that the Habsburg state had been the "misfortune of the German people (10, 21);" and had exerted a "disastrous" influence upon them (2); that this state had "betrayed the needs of the people again and again (3);" and that it would cause the German people to be "dragged into the abyss (26)." He accuses the Habsburg government of wishing to attack and to destroy "Germanism (17, 27, 30, 31, 32);" of oppressing the Germans in Austria (22); of victimizing them (12); and of having no love for them (4). He expresses hostility toward the Austrian state (8, 11); and suggests that it is necessary, for the sake of the German nation (25, 33, 34), and for the sake of the German-Austrian people (10, 14; also 9) that the alliance between Austria and German be broken off (33, 34); and that the Habsburg monarchy be destroyed (9, 13, 14, 25).

Table 16. The Habsburg State

Statement Number	Statement	Source Book	Page
1	The degenerate dynasty was only too frequently confused with the people, which at the core was robust and healthy.	MK	11
2	Who could have studied German history . . . without becoming an enemy of the state which, through its ruling house, exerted so disastrous an influence on the destinies of the nation?	MK	15
3	Who could retain his loyalty to a dynasty which in past and present betrayed the needs of the German people again and again for shameless private advantage?	MK	15
4	Did we not know, even as little boys, that this Austrian state had and could have no love for us Germans?	MK	15

[16] On the basis of the data appearing above one may suggest that Hitler's assertion of a refusal, under any circumstances, to "capitulate" to the enemy (see Table 25) is based upon his tendency to view this act as a form of sexual submission.

5	The slow extermination of Germanism in the old monarchy was in a certain sense sanctioned by Germany itself.	MK	16
6	The men . . . in the Reich itself . . . as though stricken with blindness, . . . lived by the side of a corpse, and in the symptoms of rottenness saw only the signs of "new" life.	MK	16
7	The unholy alliance of the young Reich and the Austrian sham state contained the germ of the subsequent World War and of the collapse as well.	MK	16
8	The Habsburg hypocrisy, which enabled the Austrian rulers to create the outward appearance that Austria was a German state, raised the hatred toward this house to flaming indignation and at the same time--contempt.	MK	16
9	Germanism could be safeguarded only by the destruction of Austria.	MK	16
10	The House of Habsburg was destined to be the misfortune of the German nation.	MK	16
11	The consequence . . . (of my) basic insight (was) ardent love for my German Austrian homeland, deep hatred for the Austrian state.	MK	16
12	The Austrian Empire could never be preserved except by victimizing its Germans.	MK	38
13	I welcomed every development which in my opinion would inevitably lead to the collapse of this impossible state which condemned ten million Germans to death.	MK	38
14	Only (with) . . . the disintegration of (the Austrian Empire would) the hour of freedom for my German-Austrian people (arrive, and) only in this way could the Anschluss with the old mother country be restored.	MK	38
15	Men of national and patriotic mind became rebels . . . not against the nation and not against the state as such, but rebels against a kind of government which . . . would inevitably lead to the destruction of their own nationality.	MK	95
16	The Pan-German movement in German Austria . . . is to be praised for demonstrating . . . that a state authority is entitled to demand respect and protection only when it meets the interest of a people, or at least does not harm them.	MK	95
17	The Habsburgs attempted to attack Germanism with all possible means.	MK	97

18	(The Pan-German party) attacked the "exalted" ruling house . . . and . . . probed into this rotten state.	MK	97
19	(The Pan-German party) released the glorious concept of love of fatherland from the embrace of this sorry dynasty.	MK	97
20	In the field of cultural or artistic affairs, the Austrian state showed all symptoms of degeneration.	MK	123
21	An oppressive discontent had seized possession of me, the more I recognized the inner hollowness of this state and the impossibility of saving it, and felt that in all things it could be nothing but the misfortune of the German people.	MK	123
22	I was convinced that (the Austrian) state inevitably oppressed and handicapped any really great German as, conversely, it would help every un-German figure.	MK	123
23	The idea that (the Austrian) state could be maintained much longer seemed to me positively ridiculous.	MK	123
24	Austria, . . . like an old mosaic . . . had grown old and begun to crumble.	MK	124
25	Since my heart had never beaten for an Austrian monarchy, but only for a German Reich, the hour of this state's downfall could only seem to me the beginning of the redemption of the German nation.	MK	124
26	(The Germans in Austria, in embracing the Triple Alliance) helped to chain the Reich to the corpse of a state which would inevitably drag them both into the abyss.	MK	129
27	(The Germans in Austria), by virtue of (the Triple) alliance, fell more and more a prey to de-Germanization.	MK	129
28	What was the German in Austria to do if the German of the Reich recognized and expressed confidence in the Habsburg government?	MK	129
29	(If the German in the Reich . . . expressed confidence in the Habsburg government) should (the German in Austria) offer resistance and be branded by the entire German public as a traitor to his own nationality . . . when for decades he had been making the most enormous sacrifices precisely for his nationality(?)	MK	129
30	This mummy of a state allied itself with Germany (in order to promote) . . . the slow but certain extermination of Germanism in the monarchy.	MK	141

31	We were not justified in looking on, as year after year Germanism was increasingly repressed, since the value of Austria's fitness for alliance was determined exclusively by the preservation of the German element.	MK	142
32	Either we were in a pact with the Habsburg monarchy or we had to lodge protest against the repression of Germanism.	MK	146
33	I made no secret of my conviction that our catastrophic alliance with a state on the brink of ruin would also lead to a fatal collapse of Germany unless we knew enough to release ourselves from it on time.	MK	148
34	The alliance had to be broken off, the quicker the better for the German nation.	MK	149
35	It was not for the preservation of a debauched dynasty that millions had donned the steel helmet, but for the salvation of the German nation.	MK	149
36	I did not want to fight for the Habsburg state, but was ready at any time to die for my people and for the Reich which embodied it.	MK	163
37	The fantastic conception of the Nibelungen alliance with the Habsburg state cadaver has been the ruin of Germany.	MK	630
38	The rulers of Austria . . . had been . . . seeking to uphold with violence and with terrorism an independence which had been forced upon the country against the will of the people.	S-II	1451

Table 17 presents statements in which Hitler expresses his wish for the union of Austria and Germany. He expresses his belief that the destinies of these two countries are bound together (4, 5, 13); and that Austria does not wish to be separated from Germany (14). This being the case, he expresses a wish, speaking for the Germans in Austria, for the union of Austria and Germany (1, 6, 11, 12), a wish, that is to say, that Austria might "return to the great mother country (2; also 6, 7, 8, 9, 10)."

Table 17. The Union of Austria and Germany

Statement Number	Statement	Source Book	Page
1	We of the younger generation . . . have made it our life work to reunite (Germany and Austria) by every means at our disposal.	MK	3

2	German-Austria must return to the great German mother country.	MK	3
3	The German nation (must) embrace its own sons within a single state.	MK	3
4	The destiny of (the Austrian) state is so much bound up with the life and development of all the Germans that a separation of history into German and Austrian does not seem conceivable.	MK	13
5	(The) destinies (of Germany and Austria) are eternally one.	MK	13
6	The elemental cry of the German Austrian people for union with the German mother country, that arose in the day when the Habsburg state was collapsing, was the result of a longing that slumbered in the heart of the entire people--a longing to return to the never-forgotten ancestral home.	MK	14
7	The heart and memory of the best (of the German-Austrians) never ceased to feel for the common mother country.	MK	70
8	Only he who has felt in his own skin what it means to a German, deprived of the right to belong to his cherished fatherland, can measure the deep longing which burns at all times in the heart of children separated from their mother-country.	MK	124
9	I address myself to all those who, detached from their mother country . . . now, with poignant emotion, long for the hour which will permit them to return to the heart of their faithful mother.	MK	124
10	(Since my heart had . . . beaten . . . only for a German Reich) a longing rose stronger and stronger in me, to go at last whither since my childhood secret desire and secret love had drawn me.	MK	124
11	I wanted to . . . bring about the fulfillment of my most ardent and heartfelt wish: the union of my beloved homeland with the common fatherland, the German Reich.	MK	124
12	Even when Germany was prostrate in its hour of deepest distress the Austrians had wished for unity with the Reich; as Germany recovered . . . , so the longing of the Austrians for union grew.	S-II	1431
13	There had never been any separate mission for Austria:	S-II	1453

could never be such a separate mission for any German country.

| 14 | Austria did not want to be separated from the Reich. After the collapse of 1918 Austria desired to return to the Reich forthwith. | S-II | 1458 |

We may suggest, on the basis of the data appearing in Tables 16 and 17, that the complex of attitudes described therein represents a projection of the Oedipus complex[17] into social reality. Thus: Hitler advocates the destruction of the Austrian government (the father), and of the alliance between Austria and Germany (the marriage bond), in the name of the deleterious effects of these upon Germany (the mother) and the Austrian people (the son); and longs for the day when the Austrian people (the son) may be united (i. e., re-united, see footnote 17) with Germany (the mother). The entire complex, we may suggest, is embodied and summarized in the following passage:

Only (with) . . . the disintegration of (the Austrian Empire would) the hour of freedom for my German-Austrian people (arrive, and) only in this way could the Anschluss with the old mother country be restored.

(MK, p. 38)

The destruction of the father (the Austrian Empire) is perceived to be the pre-requisite for the liberation of the son (the German-Austrian people), and, consequently, for union with the mother (Germany).

5. The Individual and the Nation

Table 18 presents statements in which Hitler expresses his belief in the value and necessity of *sacrifice* in the individual's relation to the country. He stresses the importance of personal sacrifice in the name of the species (1, 2); the state (3); the community (13); and the people (15, 22, 27; see also 24). He advocates the subordination of the individual ego to the life of the community (10, 11, 14), and to the demands of Germany (26), stating, "You are nothing, your nation is everything (23)." He asks the German to work for the community (21); to be the servant of the nation (25); and to think only of the nation (28). Finally, he expresses a belief in the value of a willingness to die for the country (6, 7, 8, 9, 10, 16, 17, 17, 19, 20, 22), calling this act the "crown of all sacrifice (12)."

[17] The "Oedipal wish," however, as Hitler describes it, would appear to involve a regressive wish for union rather than a desire for sexual gratification. Thus, the emphasis, in Hitler's statements, is upon the desire of the Austrian people to "return" to a beloved, maternal object from which it has been (unwillingly) separated (see especially 17: 1, 2, 6, 8, 9, 14).

Table 18. Sacrifice

Statement Number	Statement	Source Book	Page
1	The preservation of the existence of a species presupposes a spirit of sacrifice in the individual.	MK	151
2	The sacrifice of personal existence is necessary to secure the preservation of the species.		
3	The state-forming or even state-preserving forces . . . are . . . the ability and will of the individual to sacrifice himself for the totality.	MK	151
4	A man does not die for business, but only for ideals.	MK	152
5	Only the struggle for the preservation of the species and the hearth, or the state that protects it, has at all times driven men against the spears of their enemies.	MK	153
6	The young regiments had not gone to their death in Flanders crying "Long live universal suffrage and the secret ballot," but crying "Deutschland uber Alles in der Welt."	MK	199
7	The most precious blood (in World War I) sacrificed itself joyfully, in the faith that it was preserving the independence and freedom of the fatherland.	MK	201
8	In . . . the . . . sacred . . . ground . . . the best comrades slumbered, still almost children, who had run to their death with gleaming eyes for the one true fatherland.	MK	201
9	When in the long war years Death snatched so many a dear comrade and friend from our ranks, it would have seemed to me almost a sin to complain--after all, were they not dying for Germany?	MK	204
10	The Aryan . . . willingly subordinates his own ego to the life of the community and, if the hour demands, even sacrifices it.	MK	297
11	This state of mind, which subordinates the interest of the ego to the conservation of the community, is really the first premise for every truly human culture.	MK	298
12	In giving one's life for the existence of the community lies the crown of all sacrifice.	MK	298
13	By idealism . . . we understand only the individual's	MK	298

capacity to make sacrifices for the community, for his
fellow man.

14	True idealism is nothing but the subordination of the interests and life of the individual to the community.	MK	299
15	Any man who loves his people proves it soley by the sacrifices which he is prepared to make for it.	MK	426
16	What made men die . . . was not concern for their daily bread, but love of the fatherland, faith in its greatness, a general feeling for the honor of the nation.	MK	437
17	The idea of military service now dawned on (my lads in terms of) the living consciousness of the duty to fight for the existence of our people by sacrificing the life of the individual, always and forever, at all times and places.	MK	491
18	More than once, thousands and thousands of young Germans have stepped forward with self-sacrificing resolve to sacrifice their young lives freely and joyfully on the altar of the beloved father land.	MK	631
19	To be "social" means . . . that every individual acts in the interest of the community of the people, (and to be) to such an extent convinced of the goodness . . . of this community . . . as to be ready to die for it.	S-I	15
20	To be "national" means . . . to act with a boundless and all-embracing love for the people and, if necessary, even to die for it.	S-I	15
21	Only he has a right to live who is prepared to work for the community.	S-I	62
22	The National Socialist Party looked to those idealists . . . who . . . are ready if necessary to sacrifice their own existence to the eternal life of people and of Reich.	S-I	142
23	You are nothing, your nation is everything.	S-I	402
24	Life for you . . . German boys and girls . . . must mean sacrifice.	S-I	547
25	We all are but servants in this great task of the German nation.	S-I	664
26	We would--subordinate our own ego to the demands of Germany.	S-I	664
27	Nobody can do more than sacrifice himself for his people, and to that sacrifice we must ever pledge ourselves.	S-I	664

| 28 | Let us pledge ourselves at every hour, on every day, only to think of Germany, of people and Reich, of our great nation. | S-I | 664 |

Table 19 presents statements in which Hitler expresses his sense of devotion to Germany. He expresses his love for the nation (2, 15, 16) and for the German people (1, 9); his faith in the nation (8, 9); and his "boundless loyalty to the people (12)." He indicates that he lives only for the German people (11; see also 3, 7, 15); that he is committed to serving the people (10) and to fighting "for the greatness and glory of the Reich (5);" and that, apart from Germany, he has no other "idol (2)" or "God (6)." He states, finally, that his conscience "receives its orders from one authority alone, our people (13)."

Table 19. Devotion to the Country

Statement Number	Statement	Source Book	Page
1	Our movement is . . . sustained . . . by our love for the people.	S-I	41
2	We National Socialists wish to love our Fatherland, we wish to learn to love it, to learn to love it jealously, to love it alone and to suffer no other idol to stand by its side.	S-I	68
3	We know only one interest and that is the interest of our people.	S-I	69
4	We are fanatical in our love for our people.	S-I	69
5	We became fighters for the greatness and the glory of the Reich.	S-I	253
6	We do not want to have any other God--only Germany.	S-I	367
7	During my whole political fight I have been dominated, commanded, . . . by one thought alone, Germany.	S-I	437
8	"Deutschland uber alles" is a profession of faith which to-day fills millions with a great strength, with that faith which is mightier than any other earthly might.	S-I	609
9	Our love towards our people will never alter, and our faith in this Germany of ours is imperishable.	S-I	618
10	I could, as leader, think of no more glorious, no prouder task in this world than to serve this people.	S-I	631
11	I live only for my people, and the National Socialist	S-I	634

movement thinks only of this people.

12	What it is which has made us great . . . was our boundless loyalty to our people.	S-I	662
13	This conscience of mine receives its orders from one authority alone, our people.	S-I	917
14	We know only one aim in the world: love for our German nation.	S-II	1121
15	I am interested only in the German people. To the people alone I belong and for the people I spend my energies.	S-II	1142
16	I am a German: I love and am attached to my nation.	S-II	1624

Table 20 presents statements in which Hitler expresses his sense of being united with the people. He speaks of feeling the misfortune of the people (1); of being a part of the people (2); of clinging to the people (3, 7, 10); of thinking with the people (5); of representing the people (6); of being bound up with the people (8); and of being "inseparably united" with the people (9). He expresses a desire to remain with the people (11); and a refusal to be separated from the people (12).

Table 20. Union with the People

Statement Number	Statement	Source Book	Page
1	There are thousands who with bleeding heart feel the misfortune of their people.	MK	116
2	We became . . . so much a part of the people that the people could not any longer disown us.	S-I	131
3	The National Socialist party looked to those idealists (who) cling to their people and their Reich.	S-I	142
4	I myself was and still am a child of the people.	S-I	158
5	We . . . as the Government . . . have never thought otherwise than as the people, with the people, and for the people.	S-I	425
6	I am nothing, my fellow countrymen, but the spokesman on your behalf, and I have no desire to be anything but the representative of your life.	S-I	437
7	We cling to our people . . . : we love it in all its inner many sidedness.	S-I	471

		Source	
8	Your life is bound up with the life of your whole people.	S-II	1117
9	All my strength has come from the happy consciousness of being inseparably united with my people as man and as leader.	S-II	1301
10	Man to-day refuses any longer to be separated from the life of his people; to that he clings with a resolute affection.	S-II	1438
11	Man to-day . . . will bear extreme distress and misery, but he desires to remain with his people.	S-II	1438
12	(While my) predecessor . . . looked down upon the people from above, I saw the people from within. I came from this people and I lived in it.	S-II	1456
13	Behind me stands the whole German people.	S-II	1530

Table 21 presents statements in which Hitler expresses his belief in the immortality of the German Reich. He states that "a people lives forever (14; also 12, 15);" that the Reich will "grow on into the centuries (3);" that "the party will live on (5);" and that "Germany must remain (9)." The "permanent element" of the nation (6)," according to Hitler, that which is "created for eternities (11; also 8)," is "that substance of flesh and blood which we call the German people (6; also 4, 10, 12, 13)."

Table 21. The Immortality of the Nation

Statement Number	Statement	Source Book	Page
1	The close of life is . . . not in itself the end, since there will be an endless chain of generations to follow.	S-I	190
2	Man will know that what we create will not sink into Orcon but will pass to his children and to his children's children.	S-I	190
3	This Reich . . . will grow on into the centuries. These banners shall be borne through the ages by ever new generations of our people.	S-I	208
4	The substance, a substance of flesh and blood, our nation . . . that is what is permanent.	S-I	433
5	When I shall close my eyes in death I do not know. But that the Party will live on . . . and . . . fashion the future of the German nation . . . that I know.	S-I	447

6	The permanent element is that substance of flesh and blood which we call the German people.	S-I	448
7	It is a glorious sight, this golden youth of ours: we know that it is the Germany of the future when we shall be no more.	S-I	530
8	Since we believe in the eternity of this Reich--these works of ours shall also be eternal.	S-I	593
9	Even if we must pass away, Germany must remain.	S-I	664
10	Such things (as position or standing in life) come and go. That which abides is the substance in itself--a substance of flesh and blood, our people . . . that remains, and only to that should one feel oneself to be responsible.	S-I	855
11	The individual is transitory, the people is permanent.	S-I	872
12	Men come and men die. But this community . . . it shall last for ever.	S-I	921
13	States come and States pass, but people are created for eternities.	S-I	939
14	A people lives forever.	S-II	1135
15	Status, descent, birth, position in life, property . . . all that is transitory and of little significance, when compared with the length of life of a people.	S-II	1140

On the basis of the data appearing in Tables 18-21 we may make the following interpretive comments:

(1) A willingness to be devoted to the country, to make sacrifices in the name of the country, and to subordinate one's ego to the demands of the country may be viewed as constituting the *adoption of a masochistic posture in relation to the country.* That is to say, an espousal of the attitudes described by Hitler in the preceding Tables, and a willingness to act upon them, constitutes a *masochistic relinquishment of one's own wishes* in the name of fulfilling the "wishes" of the country.[18]

(2) A wish to be "united with the people" may be viewed, in the context of previous data (see especially Table 5), as a wish that one's own body might be "welded and fused" within the substance of the national body.

(3) Hitler's belief in the immortality of the country may be viewed as

---

[18] From this point of view a willingness to engage in battle and, if necessary, to die for one's country represents, not primarily a wish to commit aggressive acts, but precisely the opposite: it is a testimony to the depth of one's devotion to the country, the *supreme act of masochistic submission.*

an aspect of his phantasy that the country is a living organism. To wit: insofar as the German people constitute the "substance" of the national body, the German Reich will continue to live as long as Germans continue to be born; that is to say, as long as "cells" are produced which can replace the "cells" which die, the national body will be "filled" with living substance and, consequently, will perpetuate itself.[19]

6. Conclusions: the Psychological Meaning of Hitler's Ideology

Table 22-a represents an interpretation of the psychological meaning of Hitler's ideology. This interpretation is based upon data appearing in Tables 1-9, and Table 21, and consists of an analysis of the relationship between Hitler's phantasies and the elements of his ideology.

Table 22-a. The Psychological Meaning of Hitler's Ideology: I

Concept	What it Represents
The country	A living organism
The people	The flesh and blood (the substance) of the national body
Politics	Efforts to maintain the life of the national body
Acting ruthlessly	Engaging in any action which serves to maintain the life of the national body
The Jew	A force of disintegration within the national body
	An organism which threatens to consume the national body
Communism	A force of disintegration within the national body
Bringing the German people together	Welding and fusing together the "cells" of the national body such that the probability of disintegration is decreased

[19] Thus, the emphasis upon "youth" in Nazi culture: young persons represent the "substance" which will constitute the national body in the future. As such, it is essential that they be infused with National Socialist ideology, i. e., trained in such a manner as to make them free of the defects and impurities which characterized the German substance in the past.

Negative conditions within the country	A disease within the national body
Improving conditions within the country	Eliminating the forces of destruction from within the national body
Saving the country	Preventing the national body from dying
The immortality of the nation	The self-renewing quality of the national body: as long as new "cells" continue to be born, they will "fill" the national body and, consequently, perpetuate it

It is clear that the elements of Hitler's ideology which appear in Table 22-a revolve around a central phantasy, which may be defined as follows: the country is a living organism, and this organism is in danger of being destroyed.

The meaning of the elements of Hitler's ideology, then, may be understood within the framework of the logic of this central phantasy. Thus: the "people" constitute the flesh and blood of this national organism; the Jew and communism represent the forces which threaten to destroy it; political action represents means whereby one attempts to "save the life" of this organism; "bringing the people together" and "improving conditions within the country" represent specific techniques whereby the effort is made to save the national body; and, finally, the "immortality" of the nation follows as a consequence of its properties as a special type of organism.

One may conclude, on the basis of this analysis, that the elements of Hitler's ideology which appear in Table 22-a are systematically related to the elements of an underlying phantasy. Further, we may suggest, the coherence of the ideology, its "logic," reflects the coherence of this underlying phantasy.

Table 22-b represents a summary and interpretative synthesis of the data appearing in Tables 9-16. The common theme which appears in this data may be described as follows: the German people are in danger of being contaminated, debased or humiliated; actions must be taken to prevent the actualization of this danger.

Table 22-b. The Psychological Meaning of Hitler's Ideology: II

Concept	What it Represents
The Nature of the Danger	
The introduction of a "poison" into the national body	The introduction of sperm into mother's body
German women will be seduced by Jews	Mother will be seduced by father

The weakness of the German people; their tendency to degrade themselves	Mother's weakness; her tendency to willingly submit to father's sexual advances
The German people will be dominated and exploited (forced to submit) by her enemies	Mother will be dominated and exploited (forced to participate in sexual relations) by father
The alliance between Germany and Austria	The (marriage) bond between mother and father

The Consequences if the Danger is Actualized

The purity of German blood is destroyed	Mother's purity is destroyed
German women are sexually contaminated	Mother is sexually contaminated
The German people debase themselves	Mother debases herself (willingly participates in the sexual act)
The German people are humiliated, their honor destroyed	Mother is humiliated, her honor destroyed (as a result of her participation in sexuality)
The destruction of Germany and "Germanism"	The destruction of mother and of her goodness

The Nature and Goal of "Rescue" Efforts

Maintain the purity of the blood	Maintain mother's purity
Prevent sexual activity	Prevent sexual relations between mother and father
Strengthen the will of the people	Strengthen mother's will (so that she will be able to resist father's sexual advances)
Persuade the people to resist oppression	Persuade mother to resist father's sexual advances
Defend the honor of the people	Defend mother's honor
Win freedom for the people	Free mother from father
Destroy the alliance between Germany and Austria	Destroy the bond between mother and father
Destroy the Habsburg monarchy	Destroy father

The frequency with which this theme appears in the data indicates that there exists a consistency in the manner in which Hitler perceives reality: wherever he looks, he observes threats to the goodness and the integrity of the German people.

Thus, a fundamental question is raised: what is the *source*, in Hitler's case, of such a perception of reality? On what basis does he determine that, indeed, the German people are threatened in such a manner?

One may ask, in the first place, if Hitler's conception of reality is rooted in systematic study; or if it represents a valid description of the external world, i. e., truth.

The answer to these questions is, simply: highly unlikely. Viewed as statements describing the external world, Hitler's major propositions--a poison is being introduced into the body of the people; the purity of German blood is endangered; German women are being seduced by Jews; the German people are weak; the German people are being dominated and exploited; an alliance with the Habsburg monarchy is destructive to Germany--are vague in meaning; often bizarre in substance; and clearly represent highly selective, personalized views. It is improbable that they are based on systematic study or observation; or that they represent a valid description of the external world. The question thus becomes: how may we account *psychologically* for such views?

We may answer this question, I believe, by viewing Hitler's perceptions as *the projection of an unconscious phantasy into social reality.*

Specifically, I would theorize, Hitler's vision of the world represents a projection of the classic, infantile complex wherein the child views the mother's participation in sexuality as "degrading," and whereby he wishes to "rescue" the mother from such participation.[20] Thus, Hitler's belief that the German people are in danger of being contaminated, debased and humiliated represents a projection of the phantasy that mother will be contaminated, debased and humiliated if she participates in sexual relations with father (the anal-sadistic conception of coitus); and Hitler's efforts to prevent this occurrence, to "rescue" the German people, represents a projection of his wish to save mother from debasement, to "rescue" her from the sexual advances of father.

[20] This complex has been described by Flugel (1931) as follows: "Since the thought of the sexual relations of the parents is, both on account of jealousy and on account of the repression of incestuous cravings, one that is usually extremely distasteful to the child, the latter often likes to imagine that the loved parent enters into such a relationship unwillingly and under compulsion. Such a belief can arise most easily in a boy's mind as regards his mother: it then in its turn gives rise to the idea of rescuing the mother from the unwelcome and tyrannical attentions of the father (p. 109)." Flugel goes on to say, "This phantasy is sometimes found too in a sublimated form in which, for instance, great enthusiasm may be aroused by the effort to deliver a small or helpless race or nation from the dominion of a larger and more powerful people, or again by the struggle for the liberation of an oppressed section of a community from the tyranny of a ruling class (p. 109)."

The infantile phantasy in which the sadistic father is perceived to be seducing and debasing the mother, then, still strongly cathected by Hitler, is projected by him, in a massive way, into social reality, and serves to transform it: everywhere Hitler perceives a "sadistic" enemy who wishes to debase the German people.

On the basis of this interpretation the following conclusions are suggested: (1) The nature and configuration of Hitler's view of social reality reflects the nature and configuration of the phantasy which is projected into it. (2) The nature and intensity of the affects with which Hitler responds to social reality reflects the nature and intensity of the affects which are bound up with the projected phantasy.

Chapter II

THE DEATH OF
HITLER'S MOTHER

l. The National Body = Hitler's Dying Mother

In the present section we wish to put forth the hypothesis that Hitler's perception of the destructive forces within the national body and of the process of deterioration occurring therein represents a projection of his perception of his mother's body as she lay dying of cancer.[21]

Thus, according to this view: the various elements of destruction within the national body--the force of disintegration; the disease; the organism which wishes to consume the nation--symbolize the cancer within Hitler's mother's body;[22] Hitler's perception of a process of deterioration occurring within Germany, and his expectation that it will culminate in the "death" of the nation, is based upon the equation of Germany's disease with the disease from which his mother suffered; and, finally, Hitler's efforts to eliminate the forces of destruction from within the national body represent a symbolic effort to remove the cancer from within his mother's body, and thereby to save her from death.

We may reconstruct the psychological process whereby Hitler comes to wish to "save the country" as follows:

Having lost his mother as a love-object, Hitler "re-finds" her in Germany. Consequently, he comes to perceive the "national body" in terms of

[21] Hitler's mother died of cancer of the breast in December, 1907, at the age of forty-eight. (Hitler, at this time, was eighteen.) An account of events surrounding this occurrence may be found in Kubicek (1954) and Kurth (1947).

[22] The following passage, in which Hitler describes the impact of the forces of disintegration upon society, may be read as a fairly accurate clinical description of the effects of cancer: "This attack is leveled against the very substance of peoples as peoples, against their internal organization. (The) attack is so embracing that it draws into the field of its action almost all the functions of life, while no one can tell how long this fight may last (S-I, pp. 692-3)."

the image of his mother's body, prior to his mother's death: as diseased, disintegrating and certain, in the absence of drastic measures,[23] to deteriorate and to die.

At this point Hitler commits himself to his life-work: to "save" Germany from death. Where his mother died, Germany shall live.[24] Where the forces of destruction attacking his mother's body could not be mastered, Hitler shall master the forces of destruction attacking Germany; where doctors were unable to cure the disease from which his mother suffered, he shall cure the disease from which Germany is suffering; and, finally, where Hitler was helpless in the face of his mother's plight, now, in the case of Germany, he shall *act*, and act decisively.

We wish to elaborate upon this interpretation in the following speculative comments.

Hitler, we may suggest, as a response to incipient loss, internalizes his mother as she lay dying. As a result, the image which is incorporated at this time is the image of *mother with cancer*, mother in the process of deteriorating from a fatal disease. Later, when the country becomes, for Hitler, a symbolic mother, the image which he has internalized, mother with cancer, becomes, in projected form, *country with forces of disintegration*, country in the process of deteriorating from a fatal disease. In other words, just as the "benign introject" (the mother) contains a malignant force within it, so does the "good country" contain malignant forces.

Hitler's task, then, at this point, is to destroy the malignancy within the national body, that is, to "separate it" from the principle of goodness (the country). The Jew, from this point of view, is the projective equivalent of mother's cancer; and Hitler's efforts to "remove" the Jew from within the

---

[23] Hitler's fanaticism, his tendency to believe that, if Germany is to recover, "drastic measures" are necessary, is rooted, we may suggest, in this tendency to equate Germany's plight with the plight of a person suffering from cancer. Thus, he justifies the necessity for political risk by comparing the nation's plight to that of a "cancer victim whose death is otherwise certain" and who would be justified in attempting an operation even if it promised "only a half a percent likelihood of cure (MK, p. 54)." And compares the plight of the nation to that of "a man who appears to have cancer and is unconditionally doomed to die" and who would be "senseless to refuse an operation because the percentage of the possibility of success is slight (HSB, pp. 40-1)." Political risk, like a risky operation, is perceived to be necessary insofar as it represents the only chance for that "heroic deed (MK, p. 57)" which can rescue a nation which is suffering from a fatal disease.

[24] Hitler's use of the term "resurrection" to describe Germany's recovery (see Table 8), we may suggest, is based upon the fact that, unconsciously, he equates this recovery with the return to life of a dead body, that is to say, with the "resurrection" of his mother. The following passage may be read in the context of this interpretation: "A homogenous national state can, by virtue of the natural inertia of its inhabitants, and the resulting power of resistance, sometimes withstand astonishingly long periods of the worst administration or leadership without inwardly disintegrating. At such times it often seems as though there were no more life in such a body, as though it were dead and done for, but one fine day the supposed corpse suddenly rises and gives the rest of humanity astonishing indications of its unquenchable vital force (MK, pp. 72-3)."

national body represent a symbolic effort to "remove" the cancer from mother's body.

Hitler's efforts to conquer the forces of destruction, however, according to the present analysis, are doomed to futility (see Chapter IV, section 1): in his unconscious, the image of mother (the country) and the image of cancer (the Jew) are inextricably bound.

Thus, insofar as Hitler is unable to relinquish his attachment to his mother, he must cling to her cancer as well. In perpetuating his love for her, he has no alternative but to love death.

2. The Denial of Death

One of the basic mechanisms underlying Hitler's behavior as a political leader, then, according to the present interpretation, is the *denial of the death of his mother.* Unable to accept the permanence of his mother's non-existence, he attempts to cause her to be "resurrected." The passage below, in which August Kubicek, Hitler's boyhood friend, describes Hitler's reaction upon learning that his mother is dying of cancer, may serve as the basis for a re-statement of the interpretation presented in this chapter.

> One morning . . . Adolf suddenly appeared in the room. He looked terrible. His face was so pale as to be almost transparent, his eyes were dull and his voice hoarse. I felt that a storm of suffering must be hiding behind his icy demeanour. He gave me the impression that he was fighting for life against a hostile fate.
>
> His eyes blazed, his temper flared up. "Incurable--what do they mean by that?" he screamed. "Not that the malady is incurable, but that the doctors aren't capable of curing it. My mother isn't even old. Forty-seven isn't an age where you give up hope. But as soon as the doctors can't do anything, they call it incurable."
>
> I was familiar with my friend's habit of turning everything he came across into a problem. But never had he spoken with such bitterness, with such passion as now. Suddenly it seemed as though Adolf, pale, excited, shaken to the core, stood there arguing and bargaining with Death, who remorselessly claimed his victim.
>
> (Kubicek, 1955, p. 82)

Hitler's "argument with death," which begins when he learns that his mother is suffering from a fatal disease, is perpetuated, we may suggest, in his struggle to prevent the death of Germany. Thus, the "bitter and passionate" speech which Hitler delivers on this occasion is the first of many which he will make. To Kubicek Hitler says, essentially, "It cannot be true that mother is going to die. She must live." To the German people Hitler says, "Germany shall not die. She must live."[25] Hitler's rage, according to this

---

[25] The following statement may be read in the context of Kubicek's account: "Therefore let no one object 'But this is impossible.' That no one can--no one must--say to me. I am not one of the men who allow themselves to say, 'It is impossible.' It must be possible. For Germany must live (S-I, p. 930)."

view, is the displaced rage of an eighteen year-old boy who refuses to accept the death of his mother. His struggle, then, constitutes a struggle against death, against a death which has already occurred and, therefore, a struggle against reality itself.

The central mechanism whereby Hitler is able to make a "struggle against death" meaningful, and therefore to perpetuate such a struggle, consists in his capacity to view death as being the result of the will of a hostile, external agency. If death is a natural occurrence, then to rage against it is futile. If, however, death is an event which is willed by a hostile agency, one may attempt to defeat death by destroying those agencies which are perceived to be responsible for it.

Hitler's rage against the death of his mother can serve no purpose. Having re-located his mother in Germany, however, Hitler attempts to put his rage to work: he shall prevent the death of the nation by defeating those who wish to destroy her.

3. Reality and Unconscious Phantasy

Earlier (Chapter I, section 6), we accounted for the nature of Hitler's perception of social reality by viewing his perceptions in terms of the *projection of unconscious phantasy.* The present data may be understood in similar terms. Here, we may suggest, Hitler's perceptions reflect his tendency to *project the image of his mother, dying of cancer, into social reality.* Insofar as such a projection is made Hitler perceives, wherever he looks, a "world in ferment;" a nation in the process of disintegration; a nation being consumed by a fatal disease.

Our present conclusions, then, are identical to the conclusions which were drawn earlier: (1) The nature and configuration of Hitler's view of social reality reflects the nature and configuration of the phantasy which is projected into it. (2) The nature and intensity of the affects with which Hitler responds to social reality reflects the nature and intensity of the affects which are bound up with the projected phantasy.

4. Summary and Conclusions

On the basis of the data and analyses appearing in the first two chapters, one may draw the following conclusions: Hitler's perception of social reality is shaped by two central phantasies, which are projected into the world. In one instance, Hitler projects an infantile, sado-masochistic sexual phantasy into social reality. Consequently, he perceives the German people to be in danger of being attacked and exploited, and of being contaminated, debased and humiliated thereby. In a second instance Hitler projects the image of his mother, dying of cancer, into social reality.

Consequently he perceives the nation to be diseased, disintegrating, and in the process of dying.

On the basis of this analysis, then, it would appear to be possible to "make sense" of Hitler's fantastic view of the world: his perceptions reflect, not a description of external reality, but a symbolic transformation of inner psychological processes. Social reality serves, for Hitler, as a "transference vehicle," providing a screen upon which his unconscious phantasies may be projected.

PART TWO

SOCIAL BEHAVIOR

Chapter III

ANTI-SEMITISM

1. The Maintenance of the "Goodness" of the German People

We have observed (Chapter I; see especially Table 19) that Hitler loves and is devoted to the German people. Here, we shall attempt to demonstrate that Hitler's anti-semitism grows out of a threat to this love, and represents a means of attempting to preserve it.[1]

Hitler's anti-semitism begins to develop, according to the present analysis, as he eavesdrops on the political discussions of his fellow construction workers in Vienna. Hitler is angered and disturbed by what he hears. He is particularly disturbed by the tendency of the workers to degrade the country, a tendency which he views, apparently, as a form of self-degradation.

> What inevitably remained incomprehensible was the boundless hatred they heaped upon their own nationality, despising its greatness, besmirching its history, and dragging its great men into the gutter. This struggle against their own species, their own clan, their own homeland, was as senseless as it was incomprehensible. It was unnatural.
>
> (MK, p. 60)

On the basis of his observations Hitler begins to experience doubt with respect to the worth of the German people; and, consequently, to question the value of his commitment to them:

> I wrestled with my innermost soul: are these people human, worthy to belong to a great nation?

[1]The analysis in this chapter is based exclusively upon Hitler's own account, which appears in Chapter II of *Mein Kampf* (pp. 37-65).

A painful question; for if it is answered in the affirmative, the struggle for my nationality really ceases to be worth the hardships and sacrifices which the best of us have to make for the sake of such scum; and if it is answered in the negative, our nation is pitifully poor in *human beings.*

On such days of reflection and cogitation, I pondered with anxious concern on the masses of those no longer belonging to their people and saw them swelling to the proportions of a menacing army.

(MK, p. 41)

Hitler's observations, then, cause a conflict to be generated within him: on the one hand, he loves the German people and wishes to devote himself toward serving them; on the other hand, he has observed behavior among them (i. e., their tendency to degrade the country) which causes him to doubt their "goodness." Insofar as Hitler's commitment to the German people is predicated upon a belief in their "goodness," his doubt in this respect causes him to question his commitment.

Hitler's efforts to resolve this conflict (i. e., to relieve the anxiety associated with the idea of becoming estranged from the people) leads him to an intensive study of the Social Democratic press. Hitler reports the results of this study:

For me immersion in the literature and press of this doctrine and organization meant finding my way back to my own people.

What had seemed to me an unbridgable gulf became the source of a greater love than ever before.

Only a fool can behold the work of this villainous poisoner and still condemn the victim.

(MK, p. 42)

The more familiar I became, principally with the methods of physical terror, the more indulgent I grew toward all the hundreds of thousands who succumbed to it.

What makes me most indebted to that period of suffering is that it alone gave back to me my people, taught me to distinguish the victims from their seducers.

The results of this seduction can be designated only as victims.

(MK, p. 44)

In proportion as the real leaders or at least the disseminators of Social Democracy came within my vision, my love for my people inevitably grew. For who, in view of the diabolical craftiness of these seducers, could damn the luckless victims.

No. The better acquainted I became with the Jew, the more forgiving I inevitably became toward the worker.

(MK, p. 63)

These passages suggest that Hitler resolves his conflict according to the following line of reasoning: since the workers do not *wish* to engage in self-degrading forms of behavior but, rather, are *forced*, to do so, the fact that such behavior exists among them is not sufficient reason to renounce a belief in their "goodness;" this being the case, one may continue to love them, and to devote oneself toward serving them.[2] In other words, insofar as the German people are helpless "victims" at the mercy of a ruthless and irresistible "seducer" Hitler is able to "forgive the worker" and, consequently, to "find his way back to the people."

2. "Separating Out" the Jew

The identification of the Social Democrats as the source of "badness" in German life does not, however, serve to permit Hitler to entirely resolve his conflict. That is to say, the Social Democrats, in spite of the special role which Hitler has assigned to them are, nonetheless, *Germans.*

Given this fact, Hitler may draw one of the following conclusions: either Germans are not *entirely good* (insofar as Social Democrats are numbered among them); or the Social Democrats are not, in actuality, Germans. Insofar as Hitler finds it necessary to believe, apparently, that the German people are "perfect," he chooses the latter conclusion.

Specifically, Hitler's resolution of his conflict is embodied in the following conclusion: the Social Democrat is not a *German;* he is a *Jew.* The Jew, that is to say, comes to represent the "foreign" element within the nation, i. e., that element which exists *within* the boundaries of the nation but which is, essentially, alien to it.

To understand the development of Hitler's anti-semitism, then, is to understand the development of Hitler's capacity to perceive the Jew as "foreign" in relation to other Germans. Here, on the basis of Hitler's own account, we shall attempt to trace this development.

Initially, Hitler does not distinguish between Jews and other Germans.

There were few Jews in Linz. In the course of the centuries their outward appearance had become Europeanized and had taken on a human look; in fact, I even took them for Germans.

(MK, p. 52)

And is repelled by the idea of anti-semitism.

The fact that they (the Jews) had, as I believed, been persecuted on this account (because of their strange religion) turned my distaste at unfavorable remarks about them into horror. . .
On grounds of human tolerance, I maintained my rejection of religious attacks in this case as in others. Consequently the tone, particularly that of the Viennese anti-Semitic press, seemed to me unworthy of the cultural tradition of a great

---

[2] It follows that, insofar as an external agency is responsible for the worker's plight the proper activity is, not condemnation of the worker, but punishment of the responsible agency. Hitler says: "In my eyes the gravest fault is no longer with him (the worker), but with all those who did not regard it as worth the trouble to have mercy on him, with iron righteousness giving the son of the people his just deserts, and stand the seducer and corrupter up against the wall (MK, p. 63)."

nation. I was oppressed by the memory of certain occurrences in the Middle Ages, which I should not have liked to see repeated.

(MK, p. 52)

In Vienna, however, Hitler begins to perceive the "foreign" characteristics of the Jew. And poses the question: "Is the Jew a German?"

Once, as I was strolling through the Inner City, I suddenly encountered an apparition in a black caftan and black hair locks. Is this a Jew? was my first thought.

For, to be sure, they had not looked like that in Linz. I observed the man furtively and cautiously, but the longer I stared at this foreign face, scrutinizing feature for feature, the more my first question assumed a new form:

Is this a German?

(MK, p. 56)

Hoping to resolve this question, Hitler studies the anti-semitic literature.

As always in such cases, I now began to try to relieve my doubts by books. For a few hellers I bought the first anti-Semitic pamphlets of my life. Unfortunately, they all proceeded from the supposition that in principle the reader knew or even understood the Jewish question to a certain degree. Besides, the tone for the most part was such that doubts again arose in me, due in part to the dull and amazingly unscientific arguments favoring the thesis.

(MK, p. 56)

But is unable to overcome his doubt and uncertainty.

I relapsed for weeks at a time, once even for months.

The whole thing seemed to me so monstrous, the accusations so boundless, that, tormented by the fear of doing injustice, I again became anxious and uncertain.

(MK, p. 56)

Gradually, however, Hitler comes to distinguish Jews from other Germans:

Since I had begun to concern myself with this question and to take cognizance of the Jews, Vienna appeared to me in a different light than before. Wherever I went, I began to see Jews, and the more I saw, the more sharply they became distinguished in my eyes from the rest of humanity. Particularly the Inner City and the destricts north of the Danube canal swarmed with a people which even outwardly had lost all resemblance to Germans.

(MK, p. 56)

And, having done so, begins to perceive that it is the Jew who is responsible for the "badness" which exists in German life. Essentially, Hitler identifies the Jew as the source of "filth" in German cultural life:

In a short time I was made more thoughtful than ever by my slowly rising insight into the type of activity carried on by Jews in certain fields . . .

What had to be reckoned heavily against the Jews in my eyes was when I became acquainted with their activity in the press, art, literature, and the theater. All the unctuous reassurances helped little or nothing. It sufficed to look at a billboard, to study the names of the men behind the horrible trash they advertised, to make you hard for a long time to come. This was pestilence, spiritual pestilence, worse than the Black Death of olden times, and the people was being infected with it! It goes without saying that the lower the intellectual level of one of these art manufacturers, the more unlimited his fertility will be, and the scoundrel ends up like a garbage separator, splashing his filth in the face of humanity. And bear in mind that there is no limit to their number; bear in mind that for one Goethe Nature easily can foist on the world ten-thousand of these scribblers who poison men's souls like germ-carriers of the worse sort, on their fellow men.

It was terrible, but not to be overlooked, that precisely the Jew, in tremendous number, seemed chosen by Nature for this shameful calling.

Is this why the Jews are called the 'chosen people?'

I now began to examine carefully the names of all the creators of unclean products in public artistic life. The result was less and less favorable for my previous attitude toward the Jews. Regardless of how my sentiment might resist, my reason was forced to draw its conclusions.

The fact that nine-tenths of all literary filth, artistic trash, and theatrical idiocy can be set to the account of a people, constituting hardly one hundredth of all the country's inhabitants, could simply not be talked away; it was the plain truth.

(MK, p. 58)

And as the agent responsible for prostitution among German women:

For the first time I recognized the Jew as the cold-hearted, shameless, and calculating director of the revolting vice traffic in the scum of the big city.

(MK, p. 59)

Finally, it would appear, Hitler is able to entirely resolve his doubt, and to affirm that, indeed, the Jew is a "foreign" people.

One thing had grown clear to me: the party with whose petty representative I had been carrying on the most violent struggle for months was, as to leadership, almost exclusively in the hands of a foreign people; for, to my deep and joyful satisfaction, I had at last come to the conclusion that the Jew was no German.

Only now did I become thoroughly acquainted with the seducer of the people.

(MK, p. 61)

Only when Hitler is able to conclude that "the Jew is no German" can he become "thoroughly acquainted with the seducer of the people." In other words, only when Hitler is able to conclude, with certainty, that the Jew is "separate" from the rest of the German people is he willing to identify the Jew, with certainty, as the source of "badness" in German life.[3]

[3] One may suggest that a circular, self-reinforcing process is operative here. That is to say, perceiving the Jew as "not German" permits Hitler to endow him with negative qualities; and, having endowed the Jew with negative qualities, it is necessary that he be "separated out" from other Germans.

3. Psychodynamics

We discussed earlier (Chapter I, section 6) the infantile complex whereby the child believes that mother participates in sexuality only because she is forced to do so by the father. We shall argue here that Hitler's attitude toward the worker represents a direct projection of this complex.

Thus: Hitler's discovery of the "self-degrading" tendencies in the worker represents a projection of his discovery of mother's participation in sexuality, and generates a tendency toward disillusionment and estrangement. And Hitler deals with this situation just as the child deals with the infantile situation: he "excuses" the worker by absolving him of responsibility. That is to say, the worker, like mother, is perceived to behave in a self-degrading manner only under the force of coercion; is perceived to be a "victim" in the hands of a diabolical "seducer."

Just as the father, then, is held responsible for the sexual behavior and degradation of the mother, so is the Jew held responsible for the sexual behavior and degradation of the German people: he is perceived to be the source of prostitution in German life; to be the seducer of German women; and to be responsible for the "filth" in German culture.

The mechanism of "separating out" the Jew may be examined in the context of this complex.

In attempting to "separate" the Jew from other Germans Hitler is attempting, we may suggest, to "split apart" the dual parental imago (mother and father in coitus). In so doing, Hitler draws a clear line of demarcation between "goodness" and "badness:" the German people (the mother) come to be the embodiment of all that is good and virtuous; the Jew (the father) comes to be the embodiment of all that is evil and immoral.[4] In place of a dual parental imago, which contains both goodness and badness (and which generates, therefore, ambivalence), Hitler attempts to create two "separate" objects: a "perfect" Germany (which generates pure love); and a "perfectly evil" Jew (which generates pure hate).

---

[4] Hitler, it would appear, identifies with the "good mother" rather than with the anal-sadistic father. The following passages suggest, however, that while Hitler disavows the *aims* of the anal-sadistic father, he affirms his *methods:* "Terror at the place of employment, in the factory, in the meeting hall, and on the occasion of mass demonstrations will always be successful unless opposed by a doctrine of equal terror (MK, p. 44)." "If Social Democracy is opposed by a doctrine of greater truth, but equal brutality of methods, the latter will conquer (MK, p. 42)." Hitler distinguishes between his own brutality and terror and the brutality and terror of his enemies, it would appear, in the following terms: while his enemies' efforts are directed toward the seduction and degradation of the people, his efforts are directed toward the *destruction of those who wish to seduce and to degrade the people.* Thus, from Hitler's point of view, he does not wish to convert the people to Nazism in order to exploit them; he wishes to win their devotion so that he might teach them to *avoid being exploited;* that he might teach them to maintain their virtue and preserve their goodness.

The Jew, then, as the embodiment of the "badness" within Germany, is the projective equivalent of the "badness" within mother's body.[5] It follows that the destruction of the Jew constitutes, for Hitler, a means whereby he may "remove the evil" from within mother's body, and thereby restore her purity and perfection.

[5] In this sense, the father is analogous to mother's cancer: he represents a *bad object embodied within a good object.*

Chapter IV

WAR[6]

1. War as a Struggle Against Death

Table 23 presents statements which indicate that Hitler believed that Germany's enemies wish to destroy the German nation. He suggests that Germany's enemies wish to annihilate her (1, 11); to cause her to disintegrate (2, 3) and to be dismembered (3); to cause her to dissolve (4, 9); to cause her to perish (5); to destroy her (6, 7, 10, 12); and to rob her of the right to live (8).

Table 23. The Enemy's Wish to Destroy Germany

Statement Number	Statement	Source Book	Page
1	Mr. Churchill's aim . . . is to annihilate . . . the German nation.	MNO	773
2	Mr. Churchill's aim . . . is to . . . disintegrate the German nation as a whole.	MNO	773
3	The real aims (of Germany's enemies) are to restore the Germany of 1648, a Germany dismembered and disintegrated.	MNO	774

[6] The analysis in this chapter is based upon data from the following sources: Hitler's *Mein Kampf* (1962) and *Secret Book* (1962); Baynes' (1942) and Roussy de Sales' (1941) collections of Hitler's speeches; and material (primarily speeches; military talks and directives; and letters) quoted by Shirer (1959). The data embodies both general expressions of attitude and belief relating to war and to national defense; and specific responses made on the occasion of events occurring prior to and during World War II.

4	The world is now striving to dissolve the German nation.	MNO	775
5	Our enemies shout today: "Germany must perish."	MNO	781
6	The British are aiming at destroying the National Socialist state, at dividing (the German people) again into their component parts.	MNO	892
7	(It was reported that Churchill said): Germany is becoming too strong for us. She must be destroyed, and I will do everything in my power to bring about her destruction.	MNO	933
8	(The enemy's) goal . . . was to rob the German nation of the most primitive right of life.	MNO	938
9	France will . . . in the future . . . attempt to dissolve Germany.	HSB	130
10	Britain was out to destroy Germany.	RF	905
11	The Allied war aim is annihilation of Germany.	RF	1418
12	The aim of (the) struggle (of the President of the United States) is to destroy one state after another.	RF	1418

Table 24 presents statements which indicate Hitler's conception of war as a *struggle for the nation's existence.* He views war as a "life and death struggle (1, 2, 7, 12, 14, 16, 18, 19, 20, 22);" as a struggle for existence (1, 3, 5, 8, 15, 24, 25, 26, 27) and for self-preservation (6, 10, 13); and as involving, for the German people, the question of "to be or not to be (4, 17; also 9, 11)."

Table 24. War as a Struggle for the Nation's Existence

| Statement Number | Statement | Source | |
		Book	Page
1	(World War I was) a life-and-death struggle before the judgement seat of history in defense of (the nation's) own existence.	MK	114
2	(In order to eliminate agitators in 1914): the Reichstach should have been dissolved, for the life and death of a whole nation was at stake.	MK	170
3	(In World War I): the German nation was engaged in a struggle for human existence.	MK	177
4	When the nations on this planet fight for existence--	MK	177

when the question of destiny, "to be or not to be,"
cries out for a solution--then all considerations of humanitarianism or aesthetics crumble into nothingness.

5	Concepts of humanitarianism and aesthetics . . . become secondary when a nation is fighting for its existence.	MK	178
6	Concepts of humanitarianism and aesthetics . . . become . . . totally irrelevant to the forms of the struggle as soon as a situation arises where they might paralyze a struggling nation's power of self preservation.	MK	178
7	(In the war of 1914): the most cruel weapons were humane if they brought about a quicker victory . . . in a life and death struggle like ours.	MK	179
8	We fight, not for theories and dogmas, we fight for the existence of the German people.	S-II	1136
9	We are fighting only for our naked beings.	MNO	704
10	Wise political leaders of a people will never see in war the aim of the life of a people, but only a means for the preservation of this life.	HSB	10
11	Even though in August, 1914 the entire German people instinctively felt that this struggle involved their being or non-being, nevertheless once the flames of the first enthusiasm were extinguished, they were not in any way clear either about the threatening non-being or the necessity of remaining in being.	HSB	76
12	For Germany these French continental-political intentions are a question of life and death.	HSB	129
13	We do not fight for systems but for a living people, that is for flesh and blood, which must be preserved.	HSB	162
14	The conflict with England is a matter of life and death.	RF	650
15	The duration of our existence is dependent on possession of the Ruhr.	RF	650
16	The war with England and France will be a war of life and death.	RF	650
17	It will no longer be a question of right or wrong but of to be or not to be for eighty million people.	RF	651
18	(Germany was preparing) for the life-and-death struggle which would then commence.	RF	681
19	(This war would be) a life and death struggle.	RF	709

20	I am aware . . . that the struggle in which I am engaging is a struggle for life and death.	RF	820
21	Nobody can avoid fighting if he does not want to go under.	RF	869
22	The conflict (will) have to be fought to a finish . . . there (is) no other solution than a life-and-death struggle.	RF	905
23	We are fighting a battle of life and death.	RF	1074
24	In the present war . . . the German people are faced with a struggle for their existence or their annihilation.	RF	1135
25	The question is . . . whether Germany has the will to remain in existence or whether she will be destroyed.	RF	1421
26	We are determined to fight for our existence with all the means at our disposal.	RF	1428
27	(These) six years of war, . . . in spite of all setbacks will one day go down in history as the most glorious and heroic manifestation of the struggle for existence of a nation.	RF	1460

Table 25 presents statements in which Hitler expresses his belief that, in spite of the efforts of her enemies to destroy her, Germany will not capitulate. He insists that Germany will permit herself neither to be forced to her knees (1); spiritually worn down (2); intimidated (4); made to waver (4); shaken (5); perplexed (5); nor driven to despair (5); and that, under no circumstances, would Germany capitulate (3, 6, 10). Rather, Germany would "secure for herself the right to live (9)," in spite of the efforts of her enemies.

Table 25. The Refusal to Capitulate

Statement Number	Statement	Source Book	Page
1	No power in the world will be able again to force us to our knees.	MNO	758
2	No power in the world . . . will . . . defeat us militarily, destroy us economically, nor spiritually wear us down.	MNO	758
3	Under no circumstances (will the world powers) experience any kind of German capitulation.	MNO	758
4	Neither terror of the moment nor the proclamation of	MNO	758

the duration of the war will intimidate us or make us
waver.

5	Ahead of us stands the eternal life of our people and nothing can shake us, perplex us, or drive us to despair.	MNO	758
6	Anything is conceivably possible except our capitulation. When it is said that this war will last three years I reply that however long it may last Germany will never capitulate.	MNO	766
7	Our hearts turn to the German nation and to the future of Germany, which we shall serve, for which we shall fight, and, if necessary, die--but never capitulate.	MNO	781
8	If they want to fight to exterminate the German nation, then they will get the surprise of their lives.	MNO	920
9	The German nation . . . will secure for itself this right to live even if thousands of Churchills and Roosevelts conspire against it.	RF	1176
10	Whatever he does, (the enemy) can never reckon on our capitulation.	RF	1418

Table 26 presents statements in which Hitler expresses his belief that the German people are unified, and will not disintegrate upon being confronted with the pressures of war. He insists that the German nation is unified (2, 6, 7, 8, 9), and that the German people are "bound and welded more strongly and more solidly together (5; also 8)." And that, therefore, in spite of the efforts of her enemies, the German people will maintain their internal solidarity (4); and will neither split up (2); go to pieces (1); nor disintegrate (3).

Table 26. Germany Will not Disintegrate

Statement Number	Statement	Source Book	Page
1	If peoples go to pieces it will not be the German people.	MNO	703
2	The German people will not split up in this fight but become more unified. If anything splits up it will be those States that are not so homogeneous.	MNO	704
3	It is infantile to hope for the disintegration of our people.	MNO	756
4	Perhaps (the war) will also be an answer to the stupidity of those in the world who believe they will be able internally to disrupt the solidarity of the German people.	MNO	758

5	We want to show (the world) how, through them, the German people are bound and welded more strongly and more solidly together.	MNO	758
6	Parties have been liquidated, trends wiped out, and one Union has been put in their place . . . we are not going to repeat the state of 1918.	MNO	779
7	If Daladier doubts the solidity of this union . . . then I answer him: . . . You are not facing different German tribes . . . , you are facing the German people . . . , (a) German nation (which) has been cured of all the temptations of international ideologies.	MNO	779
8	Nation and Army, Party and State are today one indivisible whole. No power in the world can loosen what is so firmly welded together.	MNO	934
9	The nation has become a battling unity.	MNO	940

The data presented in the preceding four Tables indicate that Hitler conceived of war as a *struggle to prevent the death of the nation.* That is to say: Hitler believes that foreign powers wish to destroy Germany. To wage war against foreign powers, therefore, is to act in such a way as to *prevent these powers from actualizing their wish,* and thereby to maintain the life (prevent the death) of the nation. The goal of war, from this point of view, is to ward off defeat, to preserve the life of the nation by repulsing those who wish to destroy her.[7]

We may suggest, further, that waging war, insofar as it constitutes an effort to prevent the death of the nation, represents a continuation of the struggle waged by Hitler in his rise to power.

We observed earlier (Chapter I, section 1) that Hitler perceives the national body to be under attack by forces which threaten to cause it to disintegrate; and that one of Hitler's central motives as a political leader is his wish to "save Germany from death." Apparently, however, in spite of the fact that he believes that his efforts to rescue Germany have been successful (Table 8), Hitler does not believe that the threat of disintegration has been eliminated thereby. Rather, having defeated the nation's *internal enemies,* Hitler's perception of the source of threats to Germany shifts to her *external enemies.* The Jews and the communists within Germany are replaced by foreign powers, particularly England (23: 1, 2, 6, 7, 11), France (23: 9), and America (23: 12) as the agencies perceived to be the embodiment of destructive forces. Thus, the struggle to "maintain the body of the people" against those who would attempt to destroy it from within (Table 2) is

---

[7] It may be observed that the term "victory" does not appear a single time in the preceding Tables.

transformed into the wish to wage a "life and death struggle (Table 24)" against those who would attempt to destroy it from without.

In the passages which appear below Hitler explicitly links the earlier struggle against internal enemies with the later struggle against foreign powers:

> Twenty-one years of a dauntless struggle for our movement have passed. After thirteen years we at last came to power. Then came years of preparation of our foreign policy, of gigantic work at home. You know that it is all an exact repetition of what happened in the Party. We asked nothing of the world but equal rights, just as we asked for the same rights at home.
>
> (MNO, p. 931)

> We are experiencing now on an international scale what we have been experiencing inside Germany in the past. When National Socialism was striving for power, its opponents, the Liberal and Democratic parties, clamored for the compulsory dissolution of the National Socialist party. In the same way the world is now striving to dissolve the German nation. By dismembering the nation they think they can deprive it of its power. That is really the aim of Great Britain and France in the present struggle.
>
> (MNO, p. 775)

> When I saw that the other side intended to fight, I naturally did that which as National Socialist of the early days, I did once before: I forged a powerful weapon of defense. And, just as of old, I proclaimed that we should be not merely strong enough to stand the blows of others but strong enough to deal blows in return.
>
> (MNO, p. 932)

Hitler, then, in waging war, perpetuates his struggle to prevent the national body from disintegrating. The field of battle and the nature of the enemy has shifted, but the purpose of the struggle is identical: to maintain the life of the national body by defeating those who are perceived as wishing to destroy it.

We may conceptualize Hitler's wish to participate in a "life and death struggle" in several other ways.

We have observed (Table 5) that Hitler attempts to overcome the forces of disintegration within Germany by causing the German people to be "welded and fused" into a compact mass. Thus, from this point of view, the belief that Germany has been "rescued from death" would be equivalent to the belief that the forces of disintegration have been conquered.

In waging war, we may suggest, Hitler is attempting to test the hypothesis that the forces of destruction have been conquered, that is, *to ascertain if the forces of unity within the national body are stronger than the forces of disintegration.* In provoking the enemy to attack, and in attempting to repulse this attack, Hitler wishes to determine if, indeed, the reconstructed national body is sufficiently "tightly knit together" such that it is able to resist the temptation to "split apart" when confronted with destructive pressure (see Table 26, especially 4, 5 and 7 in support of this hypothesis).[8]

We may suggest, finally, that participation in a "life and death struggle" represented, for Hitler, an attempt to "undo" the defeat which Germany suffered in the previous war. The statements which appear below suggest that Hitler wished to prove that, in the second struggle, "things would turn out differently," that the Germany of 1940, unlike the Germany of 1918, could not be defeated.

> There never will be another November 1918 in German history. It is infantile to hope for the disintegration of our people.
>
> (MNO, p. 756)

> This time the British face a different Germany.
>
> (MNO, p. 765)

> Germany has changed completely. Germany of today, Germany of 1940, of 1941, and of 1942 is not to be compared with the Germany of 1915, 1916, 1917, and 1918.
>
> (MNO, p. 766)

> Parties have been liquidated, trends wiped out, and one Union has been put in their place . . . we are not going to repeat the state of 1918.
>
> (MNO, p. 779)

> Nation and Army, Party and State are today one indivisible whole. No power in the world can loosen what is so firmly welded together. Only fools can imagine that the year 1918 can be repeated.
>
> (MNO, p. 934)

Where disintegration occurred in 1918 because Germany lacked internal unity, the "new" Germany, which is "one indivisible whole," will not disintegrate. Hitler "repeats" the war in the hope that he can reverse the earlier outcome: *this time* the nation shall demonstrate its capacity to survive.

2. "Protecting the Rear"

Table 27 presents statements in which Hitler expresses his belief that an important aspect of foreign policy, for Germany as well as for other nations, is the "protection of the rear."[9]

---

[8] From this point of view waging war, represents, for Hitler, a counterphobic mechanism: in his fear that destructive forces continue to be present within the national body, Hitler causes them to materialize in the form of the enemy. Having thus externalized these destructive forces, Hitler may do battle against them.

[9] Insofar as the country is a living organism, the belief that it is necessary for a nation to "protect its rear" may be viewed as a response to the perceived danger of anal-rape.

Table 27. "Protecting the Rear"

Statement Number	Statement	Source Book	Page
1	With England alone was it possible, our rear protected, to begin the new Germanic march (to obtain land . . . at the expense of Russia.)	MK	140
2	For three hundred years the history of our continent has been basically determined by the attempt of England to obtain the necessary protection in the rear for great British aims in world politics.	MK	613
3	The political separation of (America from Britain) led . . . to the greatest exertions . . . to keep the European rear absolutely covered.	MK	614
4	Bismarck . . . welcomed the Russian rear cover, which gave him a free hand in the west.	MK	656
5	If Germany wanted to defend her . . . policy against England, then she first had to seek to cover her rear with Russia.	HSB	72
6	Only when Germany's rear was completely covered by Russia could she pass over to a maritime policy which deliberately aimed at the day of reckoning.	HSB	72-3
7	(In order to gain territory in Russia): the aim of German foreign policy unconditionally had to be to free its rear against England.	HSB	74
8	France will . . . try to occupy . . . the Rhine . . . in order to be able to commit French strength elsewhere with no threat to her rear.	HSB	130
9	The rear was covered by Russia.	HSB	153
10	This covering of the rear was thought of primarily against Austria.	HSB	153
11	If . . . England had given up her neutral attitude . . . even Russia's covering of the rear would not have been able to avert an immense conflagration.	HSB	153
12	We could have utilized the year 1904. . . in a conflict with France and had Russia at our rear.	HSB	156
13	Should England nevertheless not draw any conclusions from the hard facts, then we can, with our rear secured, apply ourselves with increased strength to the dispatching of our enemy.	RF	1114

We may suggest that the belief that it is necessary for a nation to "protect its rear" is related, for Hitler, to several other beliefs, the focus of which is the necessity of "defending" the nation. We may enumerate these as follows:

It is necessary to "build up" the German nation.

> The aim (of securing the highest measure of ideal freedom) can be realized only if a single mighty German Reich exists as a shield and protection.
>
> (S-I, p. 270)

> A vast work (dealing with the) . . . safeguarding of the Reich . . . is being brought to completion.
>
> (S-II, p. 1534)

A "mighty" Germany provides assurance that those who attempt to attack Germany will "come up against a wall of iron (S-II, p. 1344-5);" and that the nation will be "impenetrable (RF, p. 681)."

It is important that a nation be large in size.

> The greater the quantity of space at the disposal of a people, the greater its natural protection.
>
> (MK, p. 136)

> In the size of a state's territory there always lies a certain protection against frivolous attacks.
>
> (MK, p. 137)

> The very size of a state offers in itself a basis for more easily preserving the freedom and independence of a people, while, conversely, the smallness of such a formation is a positive invitation to seizure.
>
> (MK, p. 137)

> Military protection already resides in the size of a territory.
>
> (HSB, p. 74)

> A certain defense against rash attacks lies in the size of a state territory.
>
> (HSB, p. 74)

These passages indicate that Hitler believed that the "larger" a state, the less susceptible it would be to enemy attacks.

It is necessary to initiate aggressive actions. Hitler's belief in the necessity of aggressive action, in this context, would appear to be related to the anticipation of attack:

> It is my conviction that the time will come when uncertainty must end: It must be possible that the German nation can live its life within the limits of its living space without being constantly molested by others.
>
> (MNO, p. 759)

And to the belief that the initiation of aggressive action is a means whereby one avoids being the passive recipient of the attacks of others:

Just as (a state without a political goal) seems exempt from an active function, in consequence of its own political aimlessness, in its very passiveness it can also just as easily become the victim of the political aims of others. For the action of a state is not only determined by its own will, but also by that of others, with the sole difference that in one case it itself can determine the law of action, whereas in the other case the latter is forced upon it. Either Germany itself tries actively to take part in the shaping of life, or she will be a passive object of the life-shaping activity of other nations. Whoever will not be a hammer in history, will be an anvil. When (the German people) believed that it could renounce the obligations of the struggle for existence it remained, up to now, the anvil on which others fought out their struggle for existence, or it itself served the alien world as nutriment. If Germany wants to live she must take the defense of this life upon herself, and even here the best parry is a thrust. In the very proportion that we let our own forces become weaker, thanks to our general political defeatism, and the only activity of our life is spent in a mere domestic policy, we will sink to being a puppet of historical events whose motive forces spring from the struggle for existence waged . . . by other nations.

(HSB, pp. 142-3)

Here, then, is a complex of related beliefs: that it is important for a nation to take measures in order to "protect its rear;" that it is necessary to "build up" the nation; to increase its size; and to initiate aggressive actions in its name. The underlying source of these beliefs, it would appear, is a conviction of the aggressive intentions of other nations, which necessitates defensive measures.

3. The Need for Territory

Table 28 presents statements in which Hitler expresses his belief that it is necessary for Germany to acquire additional territory. He speaks of the need for land (1, 2, 5); the need for soil (2, 3, 5, 10); the need for territory (4, 8, 14); and the need for "living space (8, 13; also, 12)." He expresses a wish to obtain this land in Eastern Europe (1, 10, 13, 14). And suggests that the purpose of acquiring territory is to enable Germany to obtain her "daily bread (1, 9, 11)" and to "secure her food supplies (13)."

Table 28. The Need for Territory

Statement Number	Statement	Source Book	Page
1	If land was desired in Europe, it could be obtained by and large only at the expense of Russia, and this meant that the new Reich must again set itself on the march . . . to obtain by the German sword sod for the German plow and daily bread for the nation.	MK	140

2	(The aim of German foreign policy) is to secure for the German people the land and soil to which they are entitled on this earth.	MK	652
3	The soil on which some day German generations of peasants can beget powerful sons will sanction the investment of the sons of today, and will some day acquit the responsible statesmen of blood-guilt and the sacrifice of the people.	MK	652
4	We must seek the solution of this problem . . . exclusively in the acquisition of a territory for settlement.	MK	653
5	We must . . . advance along the road that will lead this people from its present restricted living space to new land and soil.	MK	646
6	It cannot be tolerated any longer that the British nation of 44 million souls should remain in possession of fifteen and a half million square miles of the world's surface, (and that) the France nation owns more than three and a half million square miles, while the German nation with 80 million souls only possesses about 230,000 square miles.	MNO	774
7	We see that the primary cause for the existing tensions lies in the unfair distribution of the riches of the earth.	MNO	875
8	People living on an impossible soil surface fundamentally will tend to enlarge their territory, consequently their living space, at least as long as they are under healthy leadership.	HSB	46
9	War ceases to be an instrument of booty or power-hungry individuals or nations, . . . as soon as it becomes the ultimate weapon with which a people fights for its daily bread.	HSB	46
10	If today Germany seeks soil in east Europe this is not the sign of an extravagant hunger for power, but only the consequence of her need for territory.	HSB	162
11	We . . . fight . . . for a living people . . . whose daily bread must not be lacking.	HSB	210
12	Germany's future was therefore wholly conditional upon the solving of the need for space.	RF	419
13	The subject of the dispute . . . is a question of expanding our living space in the East, of securing our food supplies.	RF	649
14	The aim (of) the efforts and sacrifices of the German people in this war . . . must still be to win territory in the East for the German people.	RF	1467

An important source of Hitler's desire to acquire territory, this data suggests, is his belief that additional land and soil are necessary in order to produce foodstuffs upon which the German people may be nourished. This is stated explicitly in the following passage:

> The German nation is less in a position today than in the years of peace to nourish itself on its own territory. All the attempts . . . to bring about an increase of the German production of foodstuffs, did not enable our people to nourish itself from its own soil. In fact, the folk-mass now living in Germany can no longer be satisfied with the yield of our soil.
>
> (HSB, p. 95)

We may speculate, further, that the belief in the necessity of obtaining a food-supply is rooted in Hitler's phantasy that the country is a living organism. That is to say, if the country is a living organism, then it is necessary to feed this organism. Hitler believes, apparently, that this organism has a "large appetite," and can be nourished adequately only if Germany increases her land-mass.

4. Summary: Motives for War

Table 29 summarizes Hitler's *motives for waging war* as they have been ascertained on the basis of an analysis of his attitudes and beliefs.

Table 29. Motives for War

Motive Number	Motive
1	Wish to maintain the life of the national body by destroying those who are perceived as wishing to destroy it.
2	Wish to test the strength of the national body; to determine if it is capable of resisting the forces of disintegration.
3	Wish to "undo" the defeat suffered by Germany in the previous war.
4	Wish to "protect Germany's rear;" to defend her against attack.
5	Wish to acquire territory in order to produce foodstuffs upon which the national body might be nourished.

PART THREE

THEORY

Chapter V

IDEOLOGY AND PHANTASY

In the present work we have demonstrated a relationship between Hitler's phantasies and his ideology. That is to say, we have indicated the manner in which Hitler's phantasies, projected into social reality, come to define his beliefs and perceptions.

We may put forth, here, a further hypothesis: it is the capacity of Hitler's ideology to provide a means whereby he may express and discharge his phantasies which constitutes the *causal element in his espousal of this ideology*. The phantasy, in short, constitutes both the source of Hitler's tendency to be attracted to the ideology and the motive for his sustained interest in it.

It may be observed that this mode of explanation differs from the conventional mode of explanation whereby social scientists account for the tendency of an individual to embrace an ideology. According to the conventional view (embodied in the notion of "cultural determinism") the nature of the ideas which a man embraces reflects the nature of the ideas which are central in the cultural milieu in which this man develops.

This is not the place to develop a detailed *critique* of the notion of cultural determinism. Suffice it to say that the presence of an idea within a culture means only that there exists the *potentiality* that such an idea may be embraced; a causal explanation, in terms of this concept, is not possible. Here, we may put forth the following theory: *the central determinant of the tendency of an individual to embrace an ideology* (that is, to espouse it, invest it with psychic energy, and to exhibit a deep and sustained interest in it), *is the capacity for this ideology to provide*, for the individual, *a means whereby his phantasies might be expressed and discharged on the level of social reality*.

We may broaden this argument.

Social scientists, it would appear, have not dealt adequately with the problem of the *causes of the popularity* of an ideology within a given culture. That is to say, once an ideology has gained a degree of power within a culture, conventional modes of explanation (e. g., "group influence") may come into play as a means of explaining the *continuing power* of this ideology. These modes of explanation, however, cannot tell us *why* a given ideology has gained currency within a culture. That is to say, they cannot explain why some ideas, among all the ideas present within a culture, are "selected out" by the members of a culture and, consequently, "passed along."

According to the present theory, the central determinant of the tendency of a given ideology to gain currency within a culture is the *capacity for this ideology to provide a modus operandi for the expression and discharge of a phantasy which is shared by members of the culture*. The ideology represents, so to speak, a "shared solution," a means whereby members of the culture may, collectively, project their phantasies into social reality.[1]

---

[1] A similar point of view is suggested by Brown (1959, p. 154) and Marcus (1966, pp. 1, 247); and is implicit in Freud (1967) and Fiedler (1960).

Chapter VI

NATIONALISM

1. Introduction

Validation of the theory put forth above would depend upon demonstrations of a systematic relationship between ideology and phantasy for samples of persons who embrace a given ideology.

In the absence of such data, we shall attempt to demonstrate the *plausibility* of this theory by drawing a hypothetical picture of the manner in which elements of ideology may be related to elements of phantasy for a major Western ideology.

We shall examine, in this chapter, the ideology of nationalism, and shall attempt to reconstruct its psychological sources.[2] It is our hypothesis that the "power" of this ideology, the frequency and intensity with which it has been embraced, is a function of the "power" of an underlying phantasy, which is shared by human beings; and reflects its capacity to provide a "modus operandi" for the expression and discharge of this phantasy.

2. The Nationalist Ideology

The ideology of nationalism may be viewed as a series of "assumptions" which define the manner in which persons perceive, and act within, social reality.[3] Here, let us enumerate, and briefly discuss these assumptions.

---

[2] The theory presented in this chapter has been formulated on the basis of the following input: the findings of the present study; observations on nationalism in contemporary cultures; and the literature on nationalism (especially Kedourie, 1960; Kohn, 1944; Minogue, 1967; and Shafer, 1955).

[3] For many persons in contemporary cultures, one may suggest, the ideas of nationalism are so deeply felt, and so firmly embodied in the structure of society, that they are rarely reflected upon. As Kedourie (1960) has observed: "The doctrine (of

One's personal "condition" or "fate" is closely bound up with the "condition" or "fate" of the nation. Thus, for example, the nationalist[4] tends to assume that his own "strength," "health," "freedom" or "prosperity" is closely bound up with the "strength," "health," "freedom" or "prosperity" of the nation.

One is personally responsible for the "acts" of the nation. Thus, for example, the citizen of a nation may experience "pride" if his nation wins a war or makes a technological advance; may experience "shame" if his nation loses a war; may experience "guilt" if his nation initiates aggressive acts. The nationalist, in short, tends to react as if he himself were responsible for the "acts" of the nation, even if he has not, in reality, participated in them.

It is important to act "in the name of" the nation. The nationalist tends to attach moral approbation to actions which are directed toward the "betterment" of his country's fate or condition. Thus, a citizen of a nation is enjoined to make "sacrifices" for his country: to be willing to fight and to die for it; to act in such a manner as to preserve its "freedom;" to act in such a manner as to eliminate "negative conditions" within it.

It is natural to experience emotions, often very powerful ones, toward nations. Thus, for example, one may "love" one's country; one may "hate" it; one may be "worried about its future."[5]

It is essential that the nation be "free." The idea of freedom, as Minogue has observed (1967), tends to be associated with the belief that the nation is oppressed, or is in danger of being oppressed. Thus, for the nationalist, the idea of freedom is bound up with the idea of *liberation:* if freedom is to be won, or to be maintained, it is necessary that the tyrants who wish to oppress the nation be overthrown or eliminated.[6]

It is important for the people of a nation to be "united." Nationalists tend to believe that it is important to break down barriers separating countrymen so that persons might "come together" to constitute a unified whole.[7]

---

nationalism) holds that humanity is naturally divided into nations, that nations are known by certain characteristics which can be ascertained, and that the only legitimate type of government is national self-government. Not the least triumph of this doctrine is that such propositions have become accepted and are thought to be self-evident (p. 9)."

[4] The term "nationalist" is used, in this chapter, to refer to persons who embrace the major elements of the nationalist ideology.

[5] One may observe that persons respond, in these instances, as if the nation were a living entity.

[6] It tends to be assumed, further, that a close relationship exists between "freedom" and happiness. Thus, the nationalist tends to view the achievement of liberation as a means whereby the suffering of citizens may be eliminated, or the possibility of joy and gratification increased.

[7] Minogue (1967) has suggested that this "dream of harmony" is "the most persistent kind of dream in the literature of nationalism (p. 50)."

3. The Denial of Separateness

The country, we may suggest, constitutes a continual "presence" in the life of the individual who resides within it. That is to say, the citizen of a nation tends to perceive that he lives within the boundaries of the nation; tends to be conscious of being "a part" of the nation; and tends to be aware of, and to participate in, "national events." The country, in short, constitutes a frame, a context, in which reality is experienced. It is "there," present in the consciousness of the individual, and may be viewed as a "companion" which accompanies him through life.[8]

We may theorize that, from a psychological point of view, the country serves to enable one to *avoid perceiving that he is alone*, that is, to avoid perceiving that one is "an entity separate from all others (Fromm, 1941, p. 45)." Insofar as the country is experienced as a continual "presence" in one's life, the probability is diminished that one will become aware of oneself as a separate individual.

The nationalist's dream of "unity," in terms of this theory, represents a further aspect of the denial of separation. That is to say, if men are "together," then they are not separate entities, are not alone.

We may theorize, further, that the nation, as an idea and institution created by human beings, represents a *collective solution to the problem of separation.* Men, that is to say, responding to their shared fear of being separate and alone, invent the nation; and, in attempting to cope with this fear, they collectively cling to it.[9]

We may be more specific: the country, we may suggest, represents a *projection of the image of the omnipotent mother.* The nationalist deals with the problem of separation by imagining himself to be attached to, and contained within, a symbolic mother, the nation.[10] The country, as an omnipotent mother, is imagined to be watching over him, to be shielding him from danger.

The dream of union, from this point of view, reflects the wish that persons might be *fused together within the mother's body.* Insofar as the nation is imagined to be a real entity, it is the nationalist's wish that persons

[8] The mass-media, one may suggest, play a central role in modern nations in causing the "presence" of the country to be experienced on a day to day basis. Messages received from television, radio, and the newspaper keep one "in touch" with the country. However isolated the individual may be, in reality, contact with the mass-media provide assurance that one is connected to a larger whole.

[9] Brown (1959) has stated, in this context, that "Society was not constructed, as Aristotle says, for the sake of life and more life, but from defect, from death and the flight from death, from fear of separation and fear of individuality (p. 106)."

[10] According to Neumann (1954), "Anything big and embracing which contains, surrounds, enwraps, shelters, preserves and nourishes anything small belongs to the primordial matriarchal realm (p. 14)."

might be "snuggled together" within it, that individual bodies and identities might fuse in this giant "melting pot."

Within the framework of the present theory, then, the country embodies a *collective denial of separation from the mother.* Unable to tolerate the anxiety associated with the idea that separation from the mother is permanent, men invent, and embrace, a substitute for the mother. The nationalist says, essentially, "I am not separate from my mother: the country is my mother, and I am attached to it." Having "lost" one's original mother, men create an entity, the nation, in which they may find her once again.[11]

4. Serving the Country = Serving the Mother

Insofar as the country represents a projection of the image of the mother, the tendency to love one's country may be viewed in terms of a displacement of one's love for the mother. In the name of this love, one is willing to make "sacrifices." That is, just as the child demonstrates his love for his mother through his willingness to perform "virtuous" acts, so does the nationalist demonstrate his love for his country.

We may describe the tendency to be willing to make sacrifices in the name of the country in another way: the country comes to represent a projection of the maternal super-ego, the contents of which are defined in terms of the "problems" which are besetting the nation at any given moment. The reward for demonstrating a willingness to devote oneself to the solution of these problems is the love and benevolence of one's super-ego, that is, in projected form, a sense of being sheltered and protected by the omnipotent mother, the nation.

The country, in terms of this theory, may be viewed as an ego-ideal: it serves to define goals for the individual and to provide, for him, a sense of direction and purpose. The "meaning of life," once a wish to serve mother and so to win her love, becomes, for the nationalist, a wish to serve his nation.

5. The Country as a Projection of Infantile Narcissism

Let us introduce this section with a brief discussion of the concept of *primal narcissism.*[12]

---

[11] This may be put another way: Unable to perpetuate his containment within a real body, the body of his mother, the nationalist attaches himself to a symbolic body, the country, and imagines himself to be contained therein. (See, in this context, Brown's discussion of sublimation--1959, Chapter XII.)

[12] Material relevant to this discussion may be found in Ferenczi (1950); Freud (1962,1963); Fromm (1941, Chapters II and IV; 1964, Chapter IV); Mahler (1968, especially Chapters I and VII); and Brown (1959, Chapters IV and IX).

The child, it would appear, does not distinguish, early in his life, between his own body and his mother's body, nor between himself and the external world. Insofar as the child loves himself, then, he loves the entire world. That is, since he *is* the entire world, the child loves the world as he loves himself.

The child's experience of this early phase, it would appear, involves a sense of "narcissistic omnipotence:" he experiences himself to be complete within himself; to be perfect; to be all-powerful.

Reality, however, contradicts this "dream of narcissistic omnipotence in a world of love and pleasure (Brown, 1959, p. 113)." The individual begins to perceive, as he matures, that he is not "at one" with his mother's body; that his own ego is separate from the external world; that he is finite. Gradually, narcissistic phantasies come to be deflated as one is forced to confront the reality of weakness, imperfection and human limitations.

It would appear, however, that our narcissistic dreams are not abandoned.[13] While renounced, ostensibly, in the name of an adjustment to reality, we continue to harbor these dreams within, to imagine that, one day, our perfect world shall return.

The idea of the country, we may suggest, may be understood in terms of this concept.

Specifically, we may theorize, the country, as an idea and institution, grows out of the *wish to recapture, and to perpetuate, the primal narcissistic dream.* The nation, that is to say, may be viewed as a projection of our narcissistic ego: it is of immense size; it is "great;" "powerful;" "beautiful." Through identification with the country, then, we attempt to incorporate its qualities, and thus to *restore our lost omnipotence.*

The nation, according to this view, represents an *externalization of our shared narcissistic phantasies.* Our dreams of greatness, power, and perfection come to be embodied in a collective ideal, which exists "out there," apart from ourselves. As such these dreams may be perceived, and acted upon, on the level of social reality.

The concept of *oppression* may be understood within the framework of this theory. Specifically, we may suggest, *the oppressor is the father* who is equated with the reality principle and with the termination of infantile narcissism.[14] To be "oppressed," from this point of view, is to be forced to

[13] Brown (1959), in this context, has stated that "The ultimate aim of the human ego is to reinstate limitless narcissism (p. 46)."

[14] The equation of the father with the reality principle and with the destruction of infantile omnipotence would appear to be rooted in several factors. In the first place, the father is associated with *demands to perform* as opposed to effortless gratification. Secondly, the father, as an "interfering third party," destroys the child's illusion of the exclusivity of his bond with mother--he intrudes upon the narcissistic union, and robs it of perfection. And finally, we may suggest, the existence of the father causes the child to be forced to confront the reality of "separateness" and individuality. That is to say, as the child becomes aware of his father's existence, he must face the fact that there are "separate" beings in the world, beings who do not participate in the mother-child unity.

submit to the reality principle, that is, to be forced to submit to the father insofar as he represents the reality principle. Thus, just as the father is perceived, by the child, to be the cause of the destruction of narcissistic omnipotence, so is the "oppressor" thought to rob the nation of its goodness, and to destroy the happiness of its people.

According to the present theory, then, the wish to "liberate" the nation represents a wish to destroy the father, and, in so doing, to destroy the "oppressive" constraints of reality. Further, the achievement of "freedom" symbolizes a release from the father and from the constraints of reality and, consequently, the restoration of infantile omnipotence.

We may offer a further interpretation.

The child, it would appear, tends to perceive the bond between father and mother in terms of *anal-sadistic sexuality* (see Chapter I, section 6; and Chapter III, section 3). Thus, insofar as the child believes he is "at one" with the mother, he experiences the father's "sadistic sexual attacks" as an attack upon himself. Or, more precisely, the father's "attacks" are perceived as an attack upon the mother-child unity, upon "goodness" itself.

The "oppressor," in terms of this theory, symbolizes the *anal-sadistic father who wishes to attack the narcissistic mother-child unity* (the nation), and to destroy it. Thus, the wish to "defend" the nation or to "liberate" it represents a wish to defend or preserve narcissistic goodness, that is, to prevent it from being "contaminated" by the anal-sadistic attacks of the father.[15]

6. "Save the Country"

The following pattern of belief is commonly expressed among nationalists: the country is "sick," or dying, or "falling apart;" it is necessary, if one is to "save the country," that constructive actions be taken by its citizens.

The meaning of this pattern of belief may be understood, I believe, within the framework of the theory presented in the previous section.

The belief that the country is sick or dying, we may theorize, reflects the *intrusion of reality into the nationalist's world of narcissistic goodness and perfection.* That is to say, such a perception of the nation reflects the emergence of the perception, for the nationalist, of the existence of "badness" within the boundaries of the nation. We may describe the hypothetical psychological process underlying the development of this belief as follows:

Since the nation represent a projection of infantile narcissism, the nationalist tends to idealize that which is contained within its boundaries: its landscape is "beautiful;" its people are good; its government is good; the

---

[15] According to this view, a fundamental motive underlying aggressive acts which are performed in the name of the country is the *wish to eliminate persons or social entities which, as symbols of the anal-sadistic father, are perceived as wishing to attack or to destroy narcissistic goodness.*

"way of life" is good. Reality, however, begins to intrude upon this narcissistically colored vision of the world: there may be ugliness in the environment; the people of the nation may be hostile or ignorant; its government may be dishonest or inefficient; the way of life may be less than ideal. To put this more broadly: The perception, on the part of the nationalist, of the existence of "badness" within the boundaries of the nation contradicts the narcissistic dream, and causes its erosion.

The belief that the country is sick or dying, then, represents an *erosion of the dream of narcissistic omnipotence.* What is "dying" when the nation is perceived to be dying is the nationalist's belief in perfection, in purity, in power.

It follows, from this point of view, that the wish to "save the nation" represents a wish to *restore infantile omnipotence*, that is, to act in such a manner that the "sickness" or "badness" within the nation is eliminated and, consequently, its perfection restored.

7. The Maintenance of the "Goodness" of the Nation

Insofar as the "badness" which the nationalist discovers within the nation is diffused throughout reality, it is impossible to eliminate. If, however, this "badness" may be localized and isolated, the conditions are created for its elimination and, consequently, for the restoration of the "perfection" of the nation.

One of the common methods whereby such localization is achieved, by nationalists, is through the *identification of "badness" with one element within the nation.* Having made such an identification, the maintenance of the "goodness" of the nation becomes contingent upon the suppression, removal or destruction of this "bad element."

In Table 30 we have listed the categories of social objects which traditionally have been identified by nationalists with "badness;" and have indicated the social phenomena which are associated with such identifications. [16]

Table 30. The Maintenance of the "Goodness" of the Nation

Element Within the Nation Which is Thought to Embody "Badness"	Resultant Social Phenomenon
The government, ruling class	Revolution
A racial minority	Racism

[16] It may be observed that various political positions may be differentiated according to the nature of the social object with which "badness" is identified. Thus, the

An ideology	Suppression of this ideology; hostility toward those who embrace it
Negative social conditions	Efforts to eliminate these conditions; the effectance of "social change"
The press	Suppression of the press

8. Summary and Conclusions

In Tables 31-a and 31-b we have summarized the interpretations presented in this chapter. The ideology of nationalism, according to the theory developed here, reflects two central phantasies: the wish to fuse with the omnipotent mother; the wish to "recapture" infantile narcissism.

Table 31-a. The Psychological Structure of the Nationalist Ideology: I

Concept	What it Represents
The country	An omnipotent mother
One is "part of" the country	One is connected to (not separated from) the mother
One lives "in" the country	One is contained within the mother's body
The "unity" of the nation	Citizens are fused together within the mother's body
Serving the country	Serving the mother

Table 31-b. The Psychological Structure of the Nationalist Ideology: II

Concept	What it Represents
The country	A projection of infantile narcissism
The oppression of the nation	Efforts to destroy the narcissistic ideal
The oppressor	The father, who acts to destroy the narcissistic ideal

"left-wing" position is associated with the identification of the government or the ruling class as the source of badness; the "right-wing" position is associated with the identification of a racial minority, foreign ideology, or the press as the source of badness; while the "liberal" position, finally, is associated with the tendency to identify badness with negative social conditions existing within the nation.

Liberation	The elimination of the father
Freedom	The recovery of narcissistic omnipotence
The country is sick, dying	A belief that the narcissistic ideal is eroding
Save the country	Restore the narcissistic ideal

It is our view that the "power" of the ideology of nationalism, its tendency to be embraced and to be perpetuated, is a function of the "power" of these phantasies; and reflects its capacity to provide a "modus operandi" whereby these phantasies might be expressed and discharged on the level of social reality.

APPENDIX

BIBLIOGRAPHY

INDEX

APPENDIX

Table A-1. The "Togetherness" of the German People

Statement Number	Statement	Source Book	Page
1	Do we not all belong together?	MK	7
2	You come into this city . . . (so that) you may gain the feeling that now we are together; we are with him and he with us.	S-I	207
3	The belief in our people . . . has joined us together into one whole.	S-I	207
4	The German people must learn to know each other again.	S-I	264
5	The millions who have been split up into professions and kept apart by artificial class distinction . . . must find once more the way to each other.	S-I	264
6	We wish to extend the hand to each other and we wish to maintain the loyalty, the great community which in olden days we praised in our people.	S-I	283
7	I will never allow anyone to divide this people once more into religious camps, each fighting the other.	S-I	392
8	For the German as a society these buildings will inspire a proud consciousness that each and all belong together.	S-I	594
9	The young live with one another, they march together, they sing in common the songs of the Movement and of the Fatherland.	S-I	628

10	If a people is rent asunder, split up in classes, . . . then (they) should realize the harmfulness of such a condition . . . (and) should come to stand together, men of all ranks, all occupations, all classes, all walks of life, and form one column of the march.	S-I	634
11	Here stand the Front of the German people--workers, farmers, and those who are creators in the sphere of the intellect--one great indestructible community.	S-I	680
12	The aim of organization is to bring folk, with all their differences, together in order that they may be able to act in common.	S-I	895
13	We must live with one another.	S-I	941
14	Our German community of the people . . . is the condition for the practical conduct of our life-struggle.	S-I	941
15	The men of Germany must draw to each other again, and must learn how to sit around the same table.	S-I	945
16	The pre-condition for relieving the distress in Germany is the restoration of the consciousness of belonging together.	S-II	1134

BIBLIOGRAPHY

Baynes, N. H. *The Speeches of Adolf Hitler*, April 1922-August 1939. Two volumes. New York: Oxford University Press, 1942

Brown, N. O. *Life Against Death*. Middletown, Connecticut: Wesleyan University Press, 1959

Ferenczi, S. Stages in the Development of the Sense of Reality in *Sex and Psychoanalysis*. New York: Basic Books, 1950

Fiedler, L. A. *Love and Death in the American Novel*. New York: Criterion Books, 1960

Flugel, J. C. *The Psychoanalytic Study of the Family*. London: Hogarth Press, 1931

Flugel, J. C. The Death Instinct, Homeostasis and Allied Concepts. *International Journal of Psychoanalysis*, Vol. 34, 1953

Freud, S. *Beyond the Pleasure Principle*. New York: Bantam Books, 1959

Freud, S. *Civilization and Its Discontents*. New York: W. W. Norton and Company, 1962

Freud, S. *The Future of an Illusion*. New York: Doubleday and Company, 1957

Freud, S. On Narcissism: An Introduction in *General Psychological Theory*. New York, Collier Books, 1963

Freud, S. *An Outline of Psychoanalysis*. New York: W. W. Norton, 1949

Fromm, E. *Escape from Freedom*. New York: Holt, Rinehart and Winston, 1941

Fromm, E. *The Heart of Man*. New York: Harper and Row, 1964

Hitler, A. *Mein Kampf*. Boston: Houghton Mifflin Company, 1962

Hitler, A. *Hitler's Secret Book*. New York: Grove Press, 1962

Kedourie, E.. *Nationalism*. London: Hutchinson, 1960

Kohn, H. *The Idea of Nationalism.* New York: The Macmillan Company, 1944

Kubicek, A. *Young Hitler: The Story of our Friendship.* London: Allan Wingate, 1954

Kurth, G. M. The Jew and Adolf Hitler. *Psychoanalytic Quarterly*, Vol. 16, 1947

Lampl-de-Groot, J., The Theory of Instinctual Drives in *The Development of the Mind.* New York: International Universities Press, 1965

Mahler, M. S. *On Human Symbiosis and the Vicissitudes of Individuation.* New York: International Universities Press, 1968

Marcus, S. *The Other Victorians.* New York: Basic Books, 1966

Minogue, K. R. *Nationalism.* New York: Basic Books, 1967

Neumann, E. *The Origins and History of Consciousness.* New York: Pantheon Books, 1954

Roussy de Sales, R., ed. *My New Order.* New York: Reynal and Hitchcock, 1941

Shafer, B. C. *Nationalism: Myth and Reality.* New York: Harcourt, Brace and World, 1955

Shirer, W. L. *The Rise and Fall of the Third Reich.* New York: Simon Schuster, 1959

INDEX